SUCCESS WITHOUT COLLEGE

Careers With Animals

Audrey Pavia

BARRON'S

All inquiries should be addressed to:
Barron's Educational Series, Inc.
250 Wireless Boulevard
Hauppauge, New York 11788
http://www.barronseduc.com

International Standard Book No. 0-7641-1621-5

Library of Congress Catalog Card No. 00-051884

Library of Congress Cataloging-in-Publication Data

Pavia, Audrey.
   Success without college : careers with animals / Audrey Pavia.
    p. cm.
   Includes bibliographical references (p.).
   ISBN 0-7641-1621-5 (alk. paper)
   1. Animal specialists—Vocational guidance.   I. Title.
SF80 .P29 2001
636'.023—dc21

                                 00-051884

Printed in Hong Kong

9 8 7 6 5 4 3 2 1

Table of Contents

Careers with Animals

The deep and profound bond that modern humans share with other animals is an ancient one. It goes back so far in time, we cannot truly pinpoint its beginning.

At first, our connection to the other creatures in our environment was one of hunter and hunted, worshipper and deity. Early humans were profoundly drawn to animals, both because they hunted them for food and because they were in awe of the skills these creatures possessed: Birds could soar high in the sky, fish could move like lightning under water, bears could kill almost any other animal with one blow of a paw, deer could disappear from sight with just a single leap.

The reason early humans were most amazed by these skills is because we did not possess them. This made animals mystical, magical creatures to be admired.

In time, humankind lost much of its awe of animals, swapping a mystical viewpoint for a practical one. Animals became primarily sources of food, clothing, and labor. Life for humans was hard, and animals made survival just a little bit easier.

With the advent of the Industrial Revolution, and most recently the Technological Revolution, the role of animals in the human world changed once again. While certain domesticated animals maintained their position as sources of food, other creatures, such as dogs, cats, and horses, suddenly had very little utilitarian use. The need for dogs to hunt vermin, herd sheep, and guard emperors dwindled. Cats no longer were necessary to keep plague-carrying rat populations down. Horses were no longer needed to get from place to place. In essence, all these jobs were taken over by machines—or eliminated altogether.

So where did this leave domesticated animals? And how about the wild animals that were once revered for their awe-inspiring skills?

Fortunately for us, all these creatures found a new place in our lives, and now their job is simply to occupy a place in our hearts. The spiritual bond that our species once had with animals so long ago is now resurfacing, in a new modern form.

If you are reading this book because you feel drawn to animals and want to be around them as much as you can, involving yourself in their lives and contributing somehow to their welfare, you are not alone. Those of us who find ourselves strongly attached to the nonhuman animals in our world have a strong desire to combine earning a living with spending time with animals. We pursue jobs in fields that concern animals, and are willing to tolerate all kinds of adverse conditions for the privilege. In many cases, these are conditions that people less connected to animals wouldn't dream of putting up with. Those of us who love animals find the time spent with these amazing creatures well worth the trade-off.

Acknowledgments

I would like to thank the following people for their assistance in writing this book:

Heidi Pavia; Randy Mastronicola; Haydee Pavia; Ron Reis; Elizabeth McCall; Cathy Blakesly; Ed Box of Maricopa County Animal Control Services; John Mays of the National Animal Control Association; Elizabeth Rosales of the Bureau of Labor Statistics; Matt Rayl of Serrano Creek Equestrian Center; Susan Ross of the California Horse Racing Board; Gayle Van Leer of Thoroughbred Services; Don Miller of The Jockey.com; Mike Maki of Premier Aquarium Service, Inc.; David Luce of the American Association of Zoo Keepers; Jim Stime of Aquarium Design, Inc.; Carol Byrnes; Danielle Willis; Celeste M. Ryfa; Elinor Gaddy; Melissa Reis; Jose Semprit; Suzie Hall; Karen MacElmurry; and Cleeve Kidd.

CHAPTER ONE

So You Want to Work with Animals?

A great many jobs exist for those whose calling it is to work with animals. Not all of these careers require a college degree, but do demand hands-on experience with animals as their primary prerequisite for being hired. For those who feel strongly bonded to the other creatures on our planet, this prerequisite is truly a blessing.

TRENDS IN THE PET INDUSTRY

A lot has changed in Western society over the past several decades, and one of these changes involves our view of pets. While the family dog was once relegated to the backyard and an occasional game of *Fetch*, he is now a cherished member of the family. The same is true of cats, who once came home only for dinner, spending most of their lives outdoors catching mice and dodging cars. Today, the family cat is more likely to be kept inside and treasured as a beloved pet.

The consequence to this change in attitude has been a burgeoning growth in the pet industry over the past 20 years; 120 million dogs and cats now reside in American households, and products and services to accommodate these pampered pets have been increasing at a steady rate. That means more jobs relating to pets—and more positions for people who love pets.

The majority of careers concerning pets that do not require a four-year college degree are hands-on jobs such as groomer, dog trainer, pet-sitter and animal control officer, to name a few. For high school graduates and career changers who don't plan to attend college but who want to spend their working time interacting directly with animals, this is good news.

TRENDS IN THE EQUINE INDUSTRY

It used to be that the horse's main function was to transport people from one place to another and pull heavy loads. With the invention of the motorized vehicle at the turn of the twentieth century, that changed. Now, the horse's primary job is one of entertainment and companionship.

Whether for racing, showing, or simply comradeship, horses represent a billion dollar industry in the United States. According to the American Horse Council (AHC), there are 6.9 million horses in the United States, including both commercial and recreational horses. A total of 725,000 of these are involved in the racehorse industry. A vast number—1,974,000—are used in showing, and 2,970,000 are simply used for recreation. Another million or so horses work for a living performing farm and ranch work, taking part in polo games, carrying police officers, and participating in other jobs.

If you love horses and enjoy being around them, you are not alone. The AHC says that 7.1 million Americans are involved in the industry as horse owners, service providers, employees, and volunteers.

The vast majority of jobs with horses do not require a four-year college degree. Rather, hands-on experience and an in-depth knowledge of equine behavior and husbandry are what's called for in most horse-related jobs. In fact, with rare exceptions, at least one or two years of solid experience in the handling of horses is required for nearly every entry-level job in the equine industry. The reason for this is simple: Horses are large and therefore potentially dangerous animals, and to be around them safely calls for practical knowledge of their behavior. It also demands a firm understanding of the rules and protocol of horse handling that have been in place for hundreds of years.

The good news is that most people who want to work with horses for a living feel this way because they have already spent considerable time around these wonderful creatures. Whether you own your own horse, have taken riding lessons for years, or simply spend every summer out in the country at your Uncle Ted's ranch, chances are you may already have the horse experience you need to get started in a horse-related career.

TRENDS IN WILDLIFE CARE

As human beings have continued to encroach on wild places, replacing open space with condos and shopping malls, the wild animals that have inhabited these lands for thousands of years are suddenly displaced. Their choices are to leave and find someplace else to live, or to try to coexist with humans. Since the amount of open land in the world is shrinking, wild creatures are finding fewer and fewer places to run to. They are forced to stay where they are despite human development, and must try to survive within urban and suburban areas that were once wilderness areas.

Unfortunately for wildlife, humans and wild creatures don't always mix: Raccoons and deer are struck by cars; sea birds get tangled in discarded fishing wire; various species are poached and poisoned; and the list goes on and on. Our cities and suburbs and even our rural areas are filled with a variety of hazards for the wild creatures that struggle to survive in and around them.

People who appreciate wildlife and have concern and compassion for individual animals want to make it their life's work to help these creatures survive in a world slowly being overrun by human civilization. Some of these individuals want to be park rangers so they can educate the public and protect the wild places that are left. Others want to work at zoos or as aquarists to watch over the exotic animals placed in their care. Still others want to rehabilitate those creatures that have met with misfortune, hopefully to make them better and return them to the wild.

Fortunately for these people, these jobs are becoming more numerous, and greater opportunities exist now than several decades ago.

The catch is that such jobs are competitive because so many people want them, and a lot of the positions call for four-year college degrees. However, there is still room in these professions for people who have put in considerable time gaining hands-on experience with wild animals, and for those who can show prospective employers that they have what it takes to get the job done.

WHAT IT TAKES

In order to be happy working in just about any job with animals, you must have certain personality traits. Loving animals and wanting to be around them just isn't enough. Without these particular traits, you won't feel comfortable in the job no matter how much you like being with animals, and you won't be much good at it either.

- *Patience and empathy.* When you are dealing with creatures that can't speak in order to verbalize their hurts and fears, patience and empathy are two vital characteristics you must possess. When animals are afraid or in pain, they act protectively, either by attacking or fleeing. You need to be able to put yourself in the animals' position and understand where this behavior is coming from so you can empathize and try to help.

Patience is an essential trait when working with animals. Often, animals do not understand what it is we want from them, whether it is to stand still for grooming, to swallow medication, or simply to follow along at the end of a rope. It takes forbearance to teach animals exactly what is expected of them, and to help them understand what *we* need to help *them*. Only a very patient person can do this effectively.

- *Willingness to learn.* When it comes to animals, you can never know enough. Just when you think you are the ultimate expert on something, a creature will come along to show you just how much you *don't* know. When working with animals, you need to keep an open mind at all times and accept the fact that you will never know everything there is to know about a particular animal or animal-related subject. Embracing this reality will enable you to keep learning throughout your lifetime of animal work.

- *People skills.* Most of the people who seek jobs with animals do so because they love to be around other sentient beings besides humans; however, this desire to be around animals can't be in place of being around people. There are virtually no animal-related jobs to be had that don't also involve dealing with humans. For this reason, people skills are an absolute necessity when working in an animal-related job.

- *Positive attitude.* A career in an animal field can be trying at times. The low pay and odd hours can wear thin sometimes, no matter how much you love your job. Because you are working with feeling creatures that are sensitive to human moods, you must strive to keep a positive, upbeat attitude at all times when dealing with your charges. A bad attitude will only illicit the same reaction in the creatures you are working with.

SALARY

If you are an animal lover, a job working day in and day out with animals is a dream come true. Also, lots of other people feel the same way you do, meaning a whole community of professional animal lovers exists out there. The downside to this, however, is that all these other animal lovers mean more job competition, and, generally speaking, the more competitive a job market is, the lower the pay.

Most people who work with animals have resigned themselves to the fact that animal careers are generally low paying, particularly for those without college degrees. It is possible to survive on the income you will earn working with animals, but only if you are willing to make some sacrifices, especially early in your career when salaries are the lowest.

- Consider living with a roommate or someone who can share expenses with you.

- Shop in discount stores for your clothing.

- Cut coupons from the newspaper for your groceries.

- Do whatever it takes to help make ends meet on a small salary.

Eventually, if you move into management or if you simply work in your chosen profession for an extended period of time, your pay will increase to a more desirable level. If you are in the type of field where starting your own business is feasible, pursue this route as a way to ultimately earn more money. In time, your salary will become more comfortable. You will most likely never get rich working with animals, but you'll have enough to survive, and rewards will come in many other forms.

LIFESTYLE

HOURS

Another aspect of working with animals that can be a bit challenging is the lifestyle that comes along with these types of jobs. A few animal professions allow you to work regular 9:00 to 5:00 hours, Monday through Friday, giving you weekends and holidays to spend with family and friends. Aquarists, for example, tend to do the majority of their work during regular business hours when their clients are also working. However, the majority of jobs with animals require working early mornings and/or evenings, weekends, and even holidays. The reason for this is that animals need to eat and be cared for at all times of the day and week, not just during the artificial weekly schedule humans have created for the majority of our work. Having a career with animals means working at times when your friends, family, and even your spouse will have time off—unless you are lucky enough to be surrounded by people who also work with animals. If not, then accept this reality before you pursue a career in the animal field. Realizing this kind of schedule comes along with the job will make it easier to tolerate when you are going through it.

TRAVEL

Something else common to animal jobs is travel. A number of animal-related professions, including park ranger, wrangler, and jockey, for example, require frequent travel. People in these jobs find it difficult to put down roots. If you are single and are looking for adventure and a way to see the country and maybe even the world, this can be a great part of the career, but if you have a family or intend to have one in the near future, all this traveling and unsettledness could be disastrous.

DANGER

Another important reality of animal-related careers is the inherent danger involved. Whether you are a groomer, a zookeeper, or a horse trainer, you are at constant risk of being injured by an animal. Dogs bite, cats scratch, and horses kick—and wildlife can inflict a lot of damage as well. If you plan to work with animals, be prepared to take your lumps now and then.

INSTABILITY

And finally, one of the most crucial lifestyle issues affecting animal workers is job instability. While many jobs with animals are very secure—veterinary technicians, equine facilities managers, and groomers tend to encounter infrequent layoffs—some positions such as zookeeper, park ranger, wildlife rehabilitator, and jockey can be tenuous. Any job that relies on public funds to pay salaries can suddenly and frequently result in layoffs, and jobs in animal-related areas that are extremely competitive and/or dependent on sensitive economic factors can be fleeting.

While lifestyle issues can make things a bit challenging for those who choose a career with animals, the rewards of working with animals more than compensate for this. Some people in these careers will gripe about job insecurity or having to work on the weekends, but few of them regret having entered the field and even fewer are willing to give it up.

PHYSICAL DEMANDS

Every career detailed in this book calls for the direct handling of animals. Some jobs require it on a constant basis (veterinary technician, farrier, wildlife rehabilitator, for example), while some on a minimal basis (equine facilities manager, aquarist, park ranger). But whatever the amount of animal handling called for in the career you choose, physical adeptness will be required.

By their very nature, most animals are fast moving and have quick responses to stimuli in their environment. Those who work with animals have to be quick too, or their charges will get the better of them. The ability to get around swiftly and easily is important for every job that calls for direct contact with animals.

Many jobs with animals also call for a strong back. Lifting, carrying, and bending are constants in many animal careers, including groomer, farrier, aquarist, zookeeper, and veterinary technician, to name a few.

For those who are employed in jobs with horses that call for riding (jockey and horse trainer are two), athleticism and overall body strength are vital.

Since concentrated animal dander is a staple in areas where mammals congregate, allergies can be a real problem for those who work with animals. If allergies to animal dander are a problem for you, you may want to stay away from the professions of groomer, veterinary technician, and zookeeper, among others—or at least discuss your plans to pursue one of these careers with your doctor. With the recent advent of a new family of allergy medications, you may be able to work in one of these careers after all, assuming your physician thinks your allergies are controllable.

If dust and hay get your nose itching and your chest wheezing, you will have trouble working around horses too. Keep this in mind if you want a job where you'll spend a lot of time at the stable.

A FEW KEY POINTS TO REMEMBER

- Society's attitudes toward animals are leading to more animal-related careers.
- Animal professionals tend to work nontraditional hours and for nominal pay.
- Certain personality traits are necessary for success when working with animals.
- Good health, a strong back, and no allergies are required of those who want to work with animals.

CHAPTER TWO

Preparing to Work

Animals are amazing creatures. First of all, they are refreshingly honest. Unlike humans, they almost always react to you solely on how you treat them, not on how you look or what you do for a living. They are also incredibly loyal. If you show them love and are able to gain their trust, you will always be special to them.

Animals are wondrous for other reasons too: They are beautiful to look at, fascinating to watch, and relaxing to be around. Their behavior and biology stimulates the mind, and their closeness to nature encourages our own spirituality.

For these reasons and more, many people seek jobs every year working with animals. What better way to earn a living than to spend your time in the company of these astounding creatures?

But before you go out and start looking for that perfect job in the animal world, you need to be prepared. The field of animal work is competitive, and only the most qualified will make the cut.

KNOWING ANIMALS

Before you set out to work with animals, it's important that you know as much as you can about the creatures you want to spend the majority of your work time with. Animals are complex, and they vary tremendously from species to species. Before you start working with animals, you need to have a thorough understanding of them—how they differ from each other and how they relate to humans.

Most people envision themselves working exclusively with mammals, specifically, domesticated ones such as dogs, cats, or horses. The appeal of these animals is profound because they not only resemble humans in their need for love and social interaction, but also because they have been bred for thousands of years to be around humans. They are particularly interactive with us, and provide much in the way of companionship.

Other people prefer to work with exotic animals, meaning wild creatures that have either been bred in captivity or were captured in the wild. Some of these animals—iguanas, parrots, and aquarium fish, for example—are kept as pets. Other exotics are kept in captivity as zoo exhibits or held temporarily in wildlife rehabilitation centers. People who prefer making a living with these kinds of creatures tend to be drawn to the uniqueness of each species, and are fascinated by complex social and biological aspects to these animals.

Before you choose the animal-related career that you wish to embark on, spend time with both domestic and wild animals in different settings in order to discover your own preferences, and to see which kinds of creatures you prefer to work with. Not only will this help you narrow down a decision, it will also provide you with some of the basic skills you will need to do the job you ultimately choose.

GAINING EXPERIENCE

While a number of the careers outlined in this book require some type of education or training, nearly all of them call for prior experience with animals before you will even be considered for a job.

For some people, this is not a problem. Many job seekers in the animal career field want to work with animals because they have spent so much time handling them in their free time that they have discovered that this is what they want to do for a living. Others have had enough contact with animals to know that they want to be around them, yet don't have significant experience handling these creatures to feel adept at it or to have something substantial to put on a résumé.

The good news, however, is that experience with animals is incredibly easy to get. You can do a variety of things to help boost your confidence handling animals and to impress a perspective employer—and have fun while you are doing it.

People who want a career working with dogs, cats, and other pets need to live with one or more of these creatures as a companion. Having a dog in your life—along with a desire to learn about the species—will do wonders in teaching you how dogs act and how they should be cared for. The same is true of cats, birds, fish, and other pets. By living with one or more of these animals while also reading up on their care and behavior and networking with other pet owners, you will gain a tremendous amount of experience that will prove valuable to you when you begin job hunting.

Another way to gain experience handling pets is to work at a local animal shelter or veterinary clinic. Not only will this look great on your résumé, but it will also prove to be a tremendous learning experience.

If it's horses you want to be around, you'll need to start doing your homework early in order to get the right amount of experience. If you already own a horse and/or have been riding for many years, you are ahead of the game. If you are a novice and are new to horses, begin by finding a good riding and horsemanship program at a local riding academy. Make sure the program will teach you not only how to ride, but also how to groom, tack up, and care for a horse. Read all the horse books you can get your hands on, and subscribe to equine magazines. Soak up as much information as you can, and spend as much time around horses and "horse people" as is humanly possible. If you have a true passion for horses, your affinity for them will blossom as your knowledge increases. In time you'll want to own or lease a horse, and will become eager to improve both your riding and equine husbandry skills.

In addition to learning to handle horses by taking formal riding and horse-manship classes, you may also want to consider volunteering in various capacities to gain more experience. Therapeutic riding programs that teach riding to the handicapped are always looking for volunteers, and prior experience with horses is usually not required. Trainers often take on volunteer grooms, and will often exchange this work for riding lessons. Stables and dude ranches also will sometimes accept volunteers to muck out stalls and help feed and water horses in exchange for riding time.

For those wishing to work with wildlife and exotic animals in a future career, experience handling wildlife is imperative. Because it is illegal to possess wildlife without state and federal permits, this experience is best gained by volunteering at a licensed local wildlife rehabilitation center and/or joining a volunteer program at a nearby zoo.

CHANGING CAREERS

If you have been working in a particular career for some time and now want to pursue an unrelated job with animals, you will have some challenges ahead of you. You will need to find time to gain the experience you'll need to make yourself viable as a full-time worker with animals. And in many cases, you will have to take some classes or training programs to meet the requirements you'll need for your new career. It's possible that you will also have to find a way to live on a lower salary, since, as discussed earlier, jobs with animals are among some of the lowest-paying work there is.

Teenagers who are still in high school and want to ultimately get a job with animals are fortunate because they can take advantage of their free time to pursue volunteer jobs where they can gain the experience they will need to get a full-time job. Career changers will have to find time to do this in between working for a living, which means doing it at night and on weekends. If you love the type of work you are ultimately pursuing, however, this should not be too much of a sacrifice. It's also a great way to make certain this is really the career you want for the rest of your life.

Career changers do have a certain advantage over those getting into these fields from scratch—prior work experience. A good many animal-related jobs call for business sense, something you may have already acquired in your previous career. If you are older, age and maturity can work to your advantage, since most employers appreciate the reliability that many adult workers possess over their younger counterparts.

FORMAL TRAINING

While the careers outlined in this book do not always require four-year degrees, nearly all of them do call for some formal training in addition to hands-on experience with animals.

Depending on the career, formal training can consist of two years at a trade school or junior college, or schooling at a specialized teaching institution for weeks or months.

If a local junior college offers a program in the career you are considering, take advantage of low tuition fees and convenient location by seeking your education there. Be certain that the program being offered is a good one and will result in a certificate or diploma program, or even an A.A. degree if warranted. Consult with the professional organization representing the field in which you wish to work (see Resources, pages 153–156) if you have questions as to whether or not a particular junior college program will give you the skills and qualifications you need to land a job in your field of pursuit.

A number of animal-related careers are also taught at proprietary trade schools that specialize in the particular field of study. Trade schools are privately owned and tend to have substantially higher tuition rates than junior colleges. The trade-off is that the programs at trade schools tend to be accelerated, meaning you will graduate a lot sooner than you would if you went to a less-expensive junior college. Job placement assistance also tends to be considerably better at trade schools than at junior colleges.

When looking for a trade school in which to enroll, there are a number of factors you should consider:

1. Accreditation. Make certain the school or program is accredited or recognized by a governing body relating to the career you have chosen. Contact a professional organization in the field you are pursuing and ask them for information on accredited schools and programs.

2. Financial Aid. If you are hoping to help pay for your education with grants and student loans, make sure the school you are considering offers financial aid assistance to its students.

3. Hands-on Training. Choose a school that uses live animals in its program, allowing you to receive hands-on training. Not only will you learn more with this type of program, but you will be more valuable to employers if they know you worked directly with animals when getting your education.

4. Tutoring. If the type of program you are considering involves academic subjects such as biology and chemistry, pick a school that provides free tutoring to its students.

5. Job Placement. The trade school you choose should help you find a job after you graduate. It should also provide internship programs since internships often lead to full-time jobs. Before enrolling, ask the admissions department to provide you with its job placement and internship statistics for the field you are interested in.

6. Quality Instructors. Before enrolling, ask about the credentials of the instructors at the school. You should be working with teachers who currently are or were previously working in the field you'll be trained in.

THE JOB SEARCH

A GOOD RÉSUMÉ

Probably the most important tool in your job hunting arsenal is your résumé. A calling card of sorts, your résumé lets potential employers know who you are, what jobs you have held in the past, and how qualified you are for the position they are trying to fill.

In most cases, a potential employer will see your résumé first, before he or she actually lays eyes on you. That is why the quality of your résumé is so important; it is basically your first impression on an employer. A good, well-put-together résumé is more likely to lead to a job interview than a résumé that is sloppy and incomplete. And since your goal is to land an interview, the quality of your résumé can make or break you.

If your writing and computer skills are good, you can easily put together a résumé on your own with the help of one of the many excellent résumé guide books on the market today. If you don't feel confident in your writing and computer skills, you would be best off hiring a service to compose and design your résumé.

Either way, be sure your résumé contains the following vital characteristics:

- *The right emphasis.* If you are a recent high school graduate with only volunteer experience and no paid job experience, be sure to play up your volunteer work. List it under the heading of "Experience," and describe the position you held, adding a parenthetical comment at the end stating that the job was of a volunteer nature. Be sure to emphasize the work you have done with animals by placing it highest on the list of jobs.

If you are a career changer, list your non-animal-related work experience in reverse chronological order under the heading of "Work Experience," and then provide a separate section for "Animal-Related Experience," including all experience (both paid and volunteer) that you have had with animals.

When including your education, be sure to place animal-related courses, diplomas, and certificates first on the list so employers are most likely to notice them.

- *Good grammar.* When writing your résumé (or looking over one that has been prepared for you), be sure the grammar is correct, and that there are no spelling mistakes. You can check this with the help of your computer by utilizing your word processing program's grammar and spell checkers, if you wrote the résumé yourself. You should also ask someone you know who has good grammar and spelling skills to read over your résumé to double-check it. Although the job you are applying for may not require much in the way of written skills, potential employers are apt to make assumptions about your intelligence based on the quality of writing on your résumé.

- *Professional appearance.* Be sure your résumé is well organized and properly formatted so it is pleasant to the eye. Try to stick to only one page, and use underlines and boldface for headings. Consider bullets and different fonts to distinguish important points. Avoid including photographs, clip art, or any other design elements since these are not appropriate for résumés.

Print the résumé on heavy stock paper—paper made specifically for résumés can be found in office supply stores—in black ink. Avoid using paper in unusual colors. Neutrals such as white, gray, and beige are the best color choices for résumés.

When mailing out your résumé, avoid folding it. Instead, mail it in a legal-size envelope, along with your cover letter.

Karen Johnson
810 Main Street
Jonesville, AK 00000
(555) 555-5555

OBJECTIVE: A position as a veterinary assistant.

PROFESSIONAL
EXPERIENCE: ***Acme Plumbing Supply, Inc., Jonesville, Alaska***
Administrative Assistant (1992–present)
Responsible for assisting office manager of plumbing supply company. Duties include answering phones, interacting with clients, maintaining computer records, filing.

Cavanaugh's, Jonesville, Alaska
Waitress (1990–1992)
Performed waitressing duties at family restaurant.

ANIMAL-RELATED
EXPERIENCE: ***Jonesville Animal Shelter, Jonesville, Alaska***
Shelter Assistant (1998–present)
Assist shelter manager two days a week. Responsibilities include

handling dogs, cats, reptiles, birds, rabbits, livestock, and other animals; cleaning cages; feeding animals. (Volunteer position)

Pet Owner
Have owned and cared for a number of different animals, including dogs, cats, horses, and iguanas.

EDUCATION: **Elksville Community College**
Certificate in veterinary assisting, 2000

Jonesville High School
Graduate, 1990

COVER LETTERS

Another important aspect to your job search is the cover letter. When answering an advertisement or posting for a job that requires a résumé be submitted, a cover letter is a necessity.

The purpose of the cover letter is to introduce yourself to the employer and call attention to your résumé. Since the cover letter will be read before the résumé is, it's important to make a good impression with this piece of paperwork.

Cover letters should be short, sweet, and to the point, and should contain the following information:

- *An introduction.* Let the reader know immediately why you are writing, that your résumé is enclosed, and where you learned of the position.

- *A synopsis.* Give a succinct overview of any volunteer experience you have that is related to animals, along with your practical work experience, if any. Make a statement that you would like to pursue a career in this field, and explain briefly why you would be the best candidate for the job.

- *A strong closing paragraph.* Thank the employer for considering you for the job, and tell him or her that you look forward to an interview. Provide a telephone number where you can be reached during business hours.

Karen Johnson
810 Main Street
Jonesville, AK 00000

November 1, 2000

Joseph Jones, DVM
Anytown Animal Clinic
800 Main Street
Anytown, U.S.A.

Dear Dr. Jones:

Attached please find my résumé for your review in response to your advertisement for a veterinary assistant in *The Anytown Gazette*.

As my résumé will attest, I have chosen a career path dedicated to working with animals in a veterinary environment. For the past three years, I have gained invaluable experience caring for animals while working as a volunteer at the local animal shelter. I also recently earned my certificate in veterinary assisting from Elksville Community College. My years as a pet owner and my experience as a shelter volunteer and veterinary assisting student have made me eager to utilize my skills in a veterinary hospital environment.

Thank you in advance for your consideration. I look forward to hearing from you soon for the purposes of scheduling an interview. I can be reached at (555) 555-5555 during the day.

Sincerely,

Karen Johnson

INTERVIEWING

If you did a good job with your résumé and cover letter, you are bound to get some interviews. While the résumé and cover letter get you in the door, it is the interview that will determine whether or not you actually get the job.

When going on interviews, keep the following points in mind:

- *Be professional.* When searching for a job in a field relating to animals, it's important to put forth a professional image. Even though the job you are applying for might involve wearing a T-shirt and jeans to work every day, you should still dress nicely for the interview, being sure to wear business attire. A businesslike demeanor and professional presentation will give prospective employers the impression that you are mature, reliable, and efficient—which, of course, you are!

Also, be sure to show up for your appointment on time. Nothing turns off an employer more than a person who is late for a job interview.

- *Be competitive.* One important factor to remember when looking for a job in an animal-related career is that positions involving animals are often in high demand. Most likely, a good number of other candidates are vying for the same job that you are, and you must find a way to stand out among them. You can do this by being well informed and knowledgeable about the position you are seeking and putting forth that knowledge in your interview. The best way to do this is by talking to a number of people who have held or now hold the same type of job you are seeking—called "informational interviewing"—before you start interviewing for jobs so you will be insightful about the field you are trying to enter.

Another way to give yourself the edge in the competition is to find out as much as you can about the organization or institution you are approaching. Try to uncover the kinds of problems they are encountering, and figure out how you can help solve those problems, then present yourself in this way in your interview. For example, if you have heard through your networking sources that a particular animal clinic is having trouble getting their technicians to sometimes step in and answer phones, make a point of letting the person doing the hiring know that you are willing to work both with the animals and in the front office, when necessary.

- *Be yourself.* It's natural to be nervous during a job interview, but don't let nerves get in the way of presenting yourself accurately to prospective employers. Try to relax before going in for your interview, and remember to just be yourself. If the job is meant to be yours, you will get it, if not, remember that another opportunity always awaits you.

- *Evaluate the employer.* While job interviews are typically thought of as a way for the employer to evaluate a prospective employee, it's also the other way around. During your interview, find out as much as you can about the job and the company so you can determine if this is the kind of place where you would like to work.

- *Follow up.* After your job interview, be certain to follow up with a thank-you note to everyone involved in the interviewing process if you are certain that you want the job. In a veterinary hospital, this might be the office manager as well as the hiring veterinarian, for example. Everyone you had contact with during the interviewing process should be officially thanked. Let these people know that you appreciated their time, enjoyed meeting them, and would love to work with them. If the choice is between you and another candidate, and you are the only one to send such a note, the scales may very well tip in your favor.

OPENING CAREER DOORS—NETWORKING

Job hunting can be a trying task. Sending out résumés, writing cover letters, going on interviews—the process can be exhausting and sometimes discouraging. But when the job you are pursuing is one you have dreamed of for much of your life, the task of job hunting is much less of a chore. For animal lovers, the possibility of working in any number of animal-related positions that might be available at any given time is bound to be an exciting prospect.

In order to increase your chances of getting a job working with animals, be sure to practice the technique of networking. When it comes to getting a job in any field, particularly those that are competitive, as animal careers tend to be, networking is a very important tool.

Networking simply means cultivating contacts within a given field. The more people you know who are involved in the career you hope to join, the better your chances of learning about job openings and ultimately getting a good position.

When you love animals, networking is easy. All you need to do is spend some time in places where professionals in the animal world congregate, and socialize with them. This means joining zoological associations if you want to be a zookeeper, volunteering at a wildlife rehabilitation center if you want to be a wildlife rehabilitator, taking on an internship at a veterinary clinic if you are studying to be a veterinary technician, hanging around at horse shows if you want to get a job as an assistant trainer. When you spend time in these places, you will naturally build bonds with the people around you because you all share something very important—a love for animals. In no time, you'll have a network of professionals in your life that you can call on when the time comes for you to start looking for a job.

A FEW KEY POINTS TO REMEMBER

- Get as much hands-on experience with animals as you can.
- Be selective when choosing a school or program for your education.
- Put forth a professional image when searching for a job.
- Use internships and volunteer experience to build a network of professionals who can help you get a paying job when you are ready.

CHAPTER THREE

Jobs with Pets

Not surprisingly, most of the people who want a job with animals are particularly interested in working with pets, specifically dogs and/or cats. These creatures have been our companions for thousands of years, and as a species, we have bonded closely with them. For someone who loves dogs and cats, a career working with these animals can be truly rewarding.

WORKING WITH COMPANION ANIMALS

Over the past few decades, our view of pets has slowly changed. People are having fewer children than they used to, and spending more time and money on their pets. While cats and dogs were once creatures that we fed once a day and lived outside most of the time, they are now considered vital members of the family. More exotic creatures such as birds, reptiles, and small mammals are also kept more commonly as pets, and are treated like part of the family too.

As a consequence of this change in viewpoint, the pet industry has grown significantly. More jobs exist working with pets than ever before. Animal lovers now have numerous opportunities to spend their workday lives alongside the creatures they love.

The type of pet-oriented job you choose should depend on what your personal aptitudes are: If you have a penchant for science and medicine, the role of veterinary technician might be for you; if you prefer to work on the outside of a pet rather than the inside, the job of groomer might be your calling; if animal behavior is your primary interest, you may have a future as a dog trainer.

Whatever your interest, it's imperative that you acquire as much experience as you can working with and handling animals before you even apply for your first job. Every pet-related career in this chapter involves hands-on involvement with pets. Familiarity in dealing with animals will be your primary form of education, regardless of the job you choose.

ANIMAL CONTROL OFFICER

About 10,000 years ago, humans adopted the notion of companion animals. Ever since then, cats and dogs have been an integral part of our society, and just as with other parts of our society, rules exist to govern and control it: Laws regarding pets help to protect people from animals and vice versa.

This is where the job of animal control officer comes in. Animal control officers are responsible for making sure that humans who keep animals as pets are following the rules. They also look out for the welfare of animals in the process. Because animal control officers help maintain order when it comes to animals in our day-to-day world, they play a very important role in our society.

The job title of animal control officer can be applied to a number of different specific jobs within specialized fields, including field operators—humane officers, cruelty investigators, livestock officers, field supervisors, rabies control/bite investigators—and shelter operators—kennel masters, operations managers, shelter managers, animal care technicians, animal care attendants, euthanasia technicians.

At one time, animal control officers were not well appreciated in the pet world. Their public image was one of a "bad guy" who went around chasing carefree mutts who were simply out to have a good time. (Films such as *Lady and the Tramp* did a lot to foster that image.) These days, however, people who care about animals understand that animal control officers are providing a valuable service by helping pets that are unwanted and neglected. Contrary to what many people think, stray animals are not out simply having a good time, and are at risk of disease, injury, starvation, and death. Animal control officers are in charge of bringing these animals in off the streets, providing them with food and shelter. While ultimately these same animals may be humanely euthanized if they do not find a home, this end is a better one than the one that awaits them on the streets.

In addition to helping animals in need, animal control officers are also responsible for enforcing public health codes, monitoring public safety as it relates to animals, and providing law enforcement services when needed.

Animal control officers are typically employed by county or local municipalities. In some states, they are authorized to carry firearms, as the job can be dangerous at times. They are required to wear uniforms, and also do their work in different environments, including an office, animal shelter, and within the community. In addition to dealing with dogs and cats, animal control officers are also expected to be able to handle horses, reptiles, birds, and other animals as situations arise.

WHAT ANIMAL CONTROL OFFICERS DO

The duties of animal control officers vary, depending on the type of job. Some duties include:

- gathering stray dogs and cats and taking them to the local animal shelter

- investigating calls regarding abused animals, stray dogs, and dog bites

- managing an animal shelter

- caring for and handling impounded animals, including reptiles

- euthanizing unadoptable, terminally ill, and/or unwanted animals

- dealing with the public

- writing reports and keeping records

- testifying in court regarding animal-related cases

- providing education to the public on animals and their care

About the Profession

- Animal control officers are employed in just about every municipality in the nation.
- The National Animal Control Association provides training and support for animal control officers around the country.
- Eight states have their own voluntary-member animal control associations.

WHAT THE JOB IS *REALLY* LIKE

The type of working conditions you will encounter as an animal control officer vary according to what type of job you have. The majority of animal control officers are involved with the community and with animal shelters, and find themselves in offices, kennels, and in private homes at various times during their work day.

For animal control officers working within the community, frequent driving is a part of job. Being outside is another aspect of working conditions, regardless of the weather.

Animal control officers involved in abuse and neglect investigations often find themselves in dirty, unpleasant, and sometimes dangerous situations.

They also have to deal with irate and uncooperative individuals who will object to having animals removed from the home, or simply resent being questioned on their animals' care.

WHY BECOME AN ANIMAL CONTROL OFFICER?

Although the job of animal control officer can be a difficult one at times, the career holds significant rewards:

- knowing you are rescuing animals in need, whether from the streets or from abusive or neglectful homes

- knowing you are helping people with problems related to animals

- being able to do a majority of your work outdoors

- having a chance to meet people in the community

- being in a position of authority

- being able to educate the public on animal issues

TRAITS YOU'LL NEED

- an affinity for all kinds of animals

- a strong emotional constitution, since you will come in contact with animals that have been abused or neglected, and will be involved in euthanizing unwanted pets

- good physical health, since animal control work often calls for strength and agility

- a thorough understanding of animal behavior

- skills at handling animals

- the ability to communicate well with people

- patience and a calm demeanor, even in stressful situations

- computer and report-writing skills

TRAINING AND CERTIFICATION

In order to get an entry-level job as an animal control officer, you'll need a high school diploma or GED. Management jobs tend to go to experienced animal control officers with college degrees, although an advanced education is not required.

When applying for an entry-level position as an animal control officer, it's advantageous to have a background handling a number of different kinds of creatures. This experience can be gained by working as a volunteer at an animal shelter before seeking a position in animal control.

On-the-job training is available for most entry-level animal control officers. The National Animal Control Association also provides continuing education for individuals already working as animal control officers.

EARNINGS

The yearly salary earned by animal control officers depends on what type of area they are working in. Entry-level positions pay minimum wage or slightly higher in just about every locale, but experienced officers who are in management or have special training can earn more. Experienced officers employed by small communities typically earn $12,000 to $15,000 a year. Midsized communities tend to pay those in management or with special training $30,000 to $40,000, while large metropolitan areas provide potential for $50,000 to $85,000 for these individuals.

A Person
Who's Done It

MEET ELINOR GADDY

VITAL STATISTICS

Elinor Gaddy wasn't quite sure what she wanted to do with her life while she was still in high school, but she knew she loved animals. After volunteering at a local humane society toward the end of high school, Elinor decided to devote her life to helping animals as an animal control officer. That was three decades ago, and she still loves her job.

Life on the Job

Q: *How long have you been working as an animal control officer?*
A: About 22 years. First, I worked for approximately three years as a field officer for the Humane Society of Missouri. I have been at St. Louis County Animal Control since July, 1981.

Q: *What made you decide to become an animal control officer?*
A: I had always loved animals and wanted to do something positive in their care and control.

Q: *What kind of education and training did you receive for this career?*
A: I'm high school educated, and have also attended training seminars sponsored by the Missouri Animal Control Association and the National Animal Control Association throughout the years.

Q: *How did you get your first job as an animal control officer?*
A: I had a high school teacher who was involved in keeping me active in school. He arranged for me to volunteer at the Humane Society every day for a half a day instead of going to classes. I was then hired to work in the adoption center and exam room.

Q: *What were your duties at this first job?*
A: I worked in various capacities, doing adoptions and kennel cleaning, and giving vaccinations, heartworm tests, etc., along with working in the Field Department.

Q: *What do you like most about being an animal control officer?*
A: I like helping people and caring for animals. I work closely with police departments and municipal governments. It makes me feel good when I can give assistance to citizens and these agencies. If you can educate people and kids, it goes a long way toward making them responsible pet owners. We regularly do educational presentations at schools, Neighborhood Watch meetings, and government functions.

Q: *What do you like least about your job?*
A: Irresponsible pet owners! Animals that are picked up may eventually be euthanized. This makes me sad and angry. I know it is a needed solution at times, but uncaring owners are the worst. It would be nice to someday not need to have animal control, but right now, this service is very much required.

Q: *Describe a typical workday for you.*

A: Our office has day and evening shifts. A recent typical day shift for me went like this: I got to the office at 8:00 A.M. and put a dog involved in a bite case into home observation for 10 days. At around 8:40, I responded to a police call for an injured dog. I brought the injured dog to our veterinarian for evaluation and treatment. Between 9:30 and 9:45 A.M. I patroled for strays. At 11:00, I did an educational school presentation for grades kindergarten through third. Between then and lunchtime, I spoke with the owner of two dogs that were running loose and issued a citation, advised the police department of a complaint about cats that were defecating in a school sandbox, and removed two bats from inside a residence.

After lunch, I picked up a loose dog and returned it to its owner, responded to an report of an aggressive dog, picked up a cat caught in a trap at a residence, checked under a front porch for a skunk, and unloaded animals and logged them into the office inventory books.

Q: *What advice would you give to people considering animal control as a profession?*

A: They should love and care about animals. It's also important to be able to get along with the public since a lot of people don't understand what we do and don't like what animal control agencies represent. If a person can do both of these things and chooses to be an animal control officer, he or she will have a job for life with many rewards.

GROOMER

If you are crazy about dogs, enjoy being around cats, and are an artist at heart, the career of professional groomer may be for you.

Professional pet groomers are responsible for making dogs look attractive by bathing, brushing, and clipping their coats. Professional groomers also bathe and brush cats (usually long-haired varieties). They spend hour after hour and day after day bathing, brushing, and clipping animals, making each coat into a work of art.

Typically, groomers are self-employed, working in their own grooming shops, in a self-owned mobile unit, or in a grooming shop where they rent space from the owner of the shop, much like hair stylists do. Some groomers, however, are employed by chain pet supply stores and work in grooming departments there. Others work for veterinarians who offer grooming as a service to clients.

While groomers deal with pets all day, they also interface with pet owners and tend to work side by side with other groomers. So they have a lot of human contact.

WHAT GROOMERS DO

The duties of a typical groomer include:

- brushing, bathing, blow-drying, scissoring, and clipping dogs

- bathing and brushing cats

- trimming toenails

- dematting and detangling neglected coats

- keeping records on clients and billing

- expressing anal glands (a distinctly unpleasant aspect of the job)

- discussing the pet's grooming needs with the owner

About the Profession

- There are approximately 25,000 to 30,000 professional groomers in the United States.
- 97 to 98 percent of groomers are female.
- The National Dog Groomers Association, the International Professional Groomers, and the International Society of Canine Cosmetologists are among several professional organizations that represent groomers.
- Approximately 60 trade schools in the United States have pet grooming programs.

WHAT THE JOB IS *REALLY* LIKE

Groomers typically work in grooming shops, which consist of a great deal of flying dog hair, hot blow-dryers, and loud clippers. The environment tends to be noisy and somewhat chaotic, although the constant presence of dogs often serves to offset the hectic atmosphere for many people.

Groomers who work in mobile units and go from home to home grooming people's pets spend a lot of time on the road.

WHY BECOME A GROOMER?

Those who groom pets for a living find great satisfaction in the job for the following reasons:

- the ability to be around pets all day

- knowing you are contributing to the pet's health and well-being

- the chance to be artistic when sculpting and scissoring coats

- an awareness that you are making pets even more attractive and lovable to their owners

- the opportunity to meet and talk to many different pet owners

TRAITS YOU'LL NEED

- an intense love of pets, particularly dogs

- experience handling dogs and cats

- an artistic flair

- good health, including a strong back

- no allergies to animal dander

- patience in dealing with sometimes uncooperative animals

- good communication skills

TRAINING AND CERTIFICATION

The majority of professional pet groomers learn their occupation by attending trade schools that specialize in grooming programs. Most of these schools require a high school diploma or GED for entrance, and will teach you how to bathe, clip, scissor, hand-strip, and trim dogs of varying breeds. Dog handling and general dog care are also included in most grooming programs, along with management training for those who want to open their own shop and hire other groomers to work for them.

Some groomers also learn the trade by working as assistant groomers, although it's easiest to get a position as an assistant groomer if you have graduated from a grooming school.

The National Dog Groomers Association, the International Professional Groomers, and the International Society of Canine Cosmetologists all provide certification for groomers. To receive certification, you must pass exams given by these organizations.

EARNINGS

Since most groomers are self-employed, it can take a while to build a clientele and start earning a regular salary. If you are renting a space in a grooming shop, you will split the fee paid on each pet you groom. Splits are typically 40 percent for the groomer, half for both groomer and shop, or 60 percent for the groomer if the groomer is very experienced and brings in his or her own clientele.

Once you are established as a groomer, you can expect to make anywhere from $30,000 to $50,000, depending on how many clients you serve. If you aspire to own your own shop and have several groomers working for you, you stand to earn a much higher salary, most likely in the six-digit range.

A Person
Who's Done It

MEET BARBARA HOOVER

VITAL STATISTICS

Barbara Hoover of Leavenworth, Kansas, walked into a grooming shop right out of high school and asked for a job—any job. A year later, after intensive hands-on training, she was grooming clients' dogs on a daily basis. Today, 13 years later, she owns her own exclusive grooming shop.

Life on the Job

Q: *What did you do prior to becoming a groomer?*
A: I was a student. I started working in a grooming shop just out of high school.

Q: *What made you decide to become a groomer?*
A: I have always had a way with animals and enjoyed working with them. I had applied at a grooming shop for any position available because I knew I would enjoy the environment. I was hired as a

bather/dryer, and the owner was kind enough to teach me grooming. I got my first job by chance. I had gone into the shop looking for any position they had open. The bather wanted to cut back on her hours, so I was able to fill that spot. I never actually made a conscious decision to be a groomer as opposed to another career; it was something I loved doing, had the talent for, and it went from there.

Q: *What kind of education and training did you receive for this career?*
A: My training came solely from the owner of the first shop where I worked. He first taught me the proper way to bathe, brush, and dry. With that came a tremendous amount of handling skills. When he thought I was ready to move up, he guided me through the grooming of his own retired show poodles. I was not allowed to groom any customer dogs until I was doing his dogs perfectly. It was probably close to a year before I met his idea of perfection.

Grooming is a career where the learning never ends. I go to dog shows to see the always changing breeds and breed standard grooming. I go to grooming seminars to see the new products and equipment that are being offered. I participate in a groomers' e-mail list where new ideas appear every day. I read any dog or cat magazine or book I can get my hands on. I try to keep up to date on any advances in animal medicine, as groomers are often the first to notice problems on clients' dogs. I also study behavior in order to understand the animals in my care.

Q: *What are the various grooming jobs you've had?*
A: I started in that first shop and worked there for 10 years. My father wanted to retire and hand over the family business to me and my husband. I quit the grooming shop to take over the business, which was not pet-related at all. But it wasn't long before my old grooming customers found me and started begging for me to groom

their dogs. I agreed to do it for many of them, and set up a small area at home. As word got around, I was doing more and more grooming and less and less office work. I finally gave in to my original love, and left the office for a home grooming shop.

In February 1999 I was contacted by a veterinary practice that needed a groomer. I met with people there and we decided to split up my week between my shop and their clinic. This is where I am today. It is two different worlds as far as grooming goes. My shop is fairly exclusive with all clients on standing four- to six-week appointment schedules. I do a lot of detailed trims, special needs animals, and some modified show trims. The veterinary clinic, on the other hand, is in a rural area where short and easy are the usual trims.

Q: *What do you like most about your job?*
A: I like the independence. Even at the clinic, I am free to do as I see fit in the grooming department. I like being able to set my own hours and work by my own schedule. I also love the artistic side, accentuating the good parts of a dog, and hiding the faults.

Q: *What do you like least about it?*
A: I have a hard time dealing with some of the owners. Unfortunately, you see a lot of neglect in this job.

Q: *What is a typical workday like for you?*
A: There's never a typical day when working with animals. It is often messy, backbreaking, hairy, smelly work—yet, I would never want to do anything else. By the end of the day, I definitely know I've been working.

Q: *What qualities do you believe a person needs to be successful as groomer?*
A: Patience! As a groomer, you also have to have a great deal of handling skills. You must know how to get the animals to trust you and want to behave for you. This is not done through discipline or

punishment, but rather through a relationship that you build with every animal that comes through the door. A heavy-handed groomer will not have better-behaved dogs. A dog that is scared because of punishment does not have enough confidence to stand up square and be still. They are the ones that are crouching down and trying to get away.

You also must have an artistic eye. You have to be able to see through all that coat at what the dog should look like, then groom accordingly. You must be able to see how taking a little off here, and more there, will balance that dog out to look its best.

A groomer should have some behavior training, and medical knowledge as well. We see most of our clients 10 or more times a year, whereas the veterinarian sees them only once. We are often the first to notice signs of illness or injuries.

Q: *What advice would you give to people considering grooming as profession?*

A: Many people believe grooming to be an easy, play-with-the-animals job. In reality, it is one of the most physically and mentally challenging jobs there is. You are using very sharp equipment on an animal that does not understand how important it is to sit still and there are always the 90-pound dogs that have never been out of the backyard, let alone heard the noise of the clippers or felt their vibrations.

My advice is to work in a shop for at least six months to a year as a bather, or cleaning or answering phones—anything that will let you see the day-to-day workings. There are a lot of groomers that quit within the first year because the job was not at all what they expected. New groomers should always work with experienced groomers. There is no way to learn all that is needed in an eight-week course. You cannot learn how to handle all of the different temperaments, breeds, or coat types in that amount of time.

SHELTER WORKER

For those who love animals, one of the sad realities of life is the need for animal shelters. Animal shelters are the orphanages of the pet world, the place where homeless pets go. In many cases, these places are just stopgaps for animals that have become temporarily separated from their owners after escaping from a yard or somehow finding themselves lost and away from home. But for the majority of pets that end up in animal shelters, the sad truth is that they are there because nobody wants them.

Animal shelters and those who staff them provide a tremendous service to the communities they serve as well as to the animals they care for. Rather than roaming the streets searching for food, making a nuisance of themselves and being at risk of injury from cars, stray dogs can be taken to a shelter where they will be given food, water, and veterinary care. Animals that are abandoned by their owners don't have to fend for themselves on the streets, but can be taken care of until they are—hopefully—adopted.

Of course, for the majority of animal shelters, euthanasia is a daily fact of life because of the sheer number of homeless animals that need care. And although it is tragic that homeless animals are put to death, it is certainly a better fate than suffering and dying out on the streets.

The people who work in animal shelters are the ones who care for homeless pets that come to the facility in need of help. Entry-level shelter workers do the majority of hands-on work with animals. They have the option of moving up to assistant shelter manager and shelter manager.

WHAT SHELTER WORKERS DO

Depending on their position within the facility, a shelter worker's job duties can include all or some of the following:

- providing food and water to impounded pets

- cleaning kennels and cages

- assisting veterinarians and veterinary technicians in the handling of all kinds of animals including reptiles and birds

- walking dogs

- evaluating animals for potential adoption

- seeking out adoptive homes

- providing adoption counseling to prospective adopters

- performing euthanasia

About the Profession

- The majority of animal shelters are run by local governments and municipalities. A smaller group of shelters are managed by private humane agencies and receive funding from government and private contributions.
- Both public and privately run animal shelters employ paid shelter workers to care for animals.
- More and more privately run animal shelters are adopting "no-kill" policies where euthanasia is not routinely performed and eligible pets are kept until adopted.
- Burnout is high among shelter workers employed in facilities where euthanasia is implemented.

WHAT THE JOB IS *REALLY* LIKE

Not surprisingly, shelter workers spend the majority of their time working inside animal shelters. Shelters can be noisy places, filled with barking dogs. They can also be malodorous at times, although properly managed shelters are cleaned regularly and unpleasant smells are kept to a minimum.

Because being a shelter worker means dealing with animals on a constant basis, contact with dirt, odor, and even parasites is part of the job. Animals that have been living on the streets are often filthy and suffering from fleas, worms, and other pests. Cleaning up these animals is often part of a shelter worker's job.

One of the greatest working-condition challenges for animal shelter workers is dealing with the realities of euthanasia. Workers employed by shelters using euthanasia must cope with death on a daily basis.

WHY BECOME A SHELTER WORKER?

Although the job can be emotionally difficult at times, there are several rewarding reasons to become a shelter worker:

- the knowledge that you are providing food, shelter, and veterinary care to animals in need

- the chance to help homeless animals find homes

- the opportunity to reunite owners with their lost pets

- the knowledge that you are providing a service to your community

TRAITS YOU'LL NEED

- an affinity for animals and motivation to help them

- experience handling animals of different kinds

- a strong emotional constitution

- good physical health

- the ability to communicate and get along with people

- typing and computer skills for office work

- willingness to work for low pay

TRAINING AND CERTIFICATION

In order to get an entry-level job as a shelter worker, you must have a high school diploma or GED. You'll also need prior experience handling animals, especially dogs and cats. Experience with other types of animals is also helpful.

A number of nonprofit organizations also provide continuing education to shelter workers. The Humane Society of the United States holds conferences and animal care expos nationwide. They also publish *Animal Shelter Magazine*, which provides educational information, and sponsor the Pets for Life Training Center in Denver, Colorado, to train shelter professionals.

The American Humane Association also offers nationwide training workshops.

INCOME POTENTIAL

Most entry-level shelter workers start out at around minimum wage, and receive gradual hourly pay increases the longer they stay in the job. Larger shelters with relatively bigger budgets start shelter workers at around $13,500. Depending on the position and whether it includes management duties, experienced workers can earn up to $40,000 a year at larger shelters.

DOG SHOW HANDLER

If you have ever watched the Westminster Kennel Club Dog Show on television, or attended a local all-breed dog show in your area, you have seen professional dog show handlers at work. Professional handlers are experts at exhibiting purebred dogs in the conformation show ring.

Professional handlers are usually self-employed individuals who work for a number of dog owner clients. The handler's job is to show the client's dog at its best advantage to the judge, and hopefully take home top honors. While many show dog owners opt to take their own dogs into the ring, many people in the dog show world believe the dogs that are handled by professionals have a better chance of winning.

Professional handlers work at dog shows of varying sizes all around the country. Breed specialty events, local all-breed dog shows, and larger, televised events are all venues for professional handlers.

Professional handlers also do more than just take dogs into the show ring for a few minutes. Owners often entrust their dogs to handlers for a certain length of time so the handler can campaign the dog at different shows; therefore, the handler is also responsible for the dog's day-to-day care.

WHAT DOG SHOW HANDLERS DO

The typical duties of the dog show handler include:

- handling dogs in the show arena; presenting them to the judge

- grooming dogs prior to showing them

- housing, feeding, and exercising dogs in their care

- conditioning and training dogs for the show ring

- traveling from show to show with the dog

About the Profession

- In the United States, an estimated 100 individuals are working full time as professional handlers.
- Thousands of dog lovers work as professional handlers on a part-time basis.
- The majority of full-time professional handlers are men.
- The Dog Handlers Guild and the Professional Handlers Association are two professional associations for dog handlers.

- The American Kennel Club recently implemented the "AKC Registered and Listed Handlers' Program," designed to promote a high standard of professionalism and better business practices among handlers, identify handlers who adhere to program standards, and to support the well-being of dogs in handlers' care.

WHAT THE JOB IS *REALLY* LIKE

Because most dog shows are held outside, professional handlers spend the majority of their time outdoors. This outdoor time also includes cleaning kennels, and feeding and conditioning dogs at home for those handlers who do not have assistants.

Professional handlers also spend a lot of time on the road, driving from show to show. Life can be lonely at times, and many full-time professional handlers are single simply because this grueling schedule makes it difficult to maintain a normal family life.

Pressure is also a part of the job for professional handlers. Every time a handler enters the dog show ring, his or her client expects a win. Since the competition is stiff at dog shows, especially with the more popular breeds, getting a win time after time can be very difficult.

WHY BECOME A PROFESSIONAL HANDLER?

- notoriety—the job of professional handler is one of the most glamorous jobs in the dog world

- being able to spend much of your time in the company of dogs

- an opportunity to travel and see various parts of the country

- the chance to meet many different people

- the likelihood of earning a good salary for full-time work

TRAITS YOU'LL NEED

- a strong affinity for dogs

- expertise at handling dogs in the show ring

- knowledge of the grooming, handling, show presentation, and breed standards of various breeds of dogs

- flair for showmanship

- patience and persistence at building a clientele

- good people skills

- readiness to travel and be away from home for long periods of time

- willingness to feed, exercise, and clean up after dogs

- desire to be self-employed and work independently

TRAINING AND CERTIFICATION

You don't need a formal education to become a professional handler, although a high school diploma or GED is recommended, along with a class or two on running a small business. It helps to be well read and knowledge-able on a variety of issues since the majority of clientele you will be dealing with are often well educated.

No special schools or programs exist to train professional handlers, although some successful pros give seminars to people who want to learn how to become better handlers.

The best way to learn the ropes of professional handling is to own your own show dog and gain experience in the show ring with your dog first. If you are successful, there's a good chance people will approach you and ask you to handle their dogs in the ring for them. You can begin building a clientele this way.

Another way to learn the ropes of professional handling is to get a job as an assistant to a professional handler. Your primary job as an assistant will be to feed, clean, and exercise show dogs in your boss' care. However, you can learn a lot by watching, and if you have talent, may even have the chance to take dogs into the ring yourself.

Once you become a working professional handler, you will want to seek recognition with the American Kennel Club's Registered and Listed Handlers' Program. To become certified with the program, you will need to provide proof of insurance coverage, appropriate kennel standards, acceptable vehicle requirements, rate schedules, sample contracts, and references. Handlers who meet the program standards are expected to maintain these standards to maintain a Registered or Listed status.

EARNINGS

Professional handlers are paid by the show. For each show the handler enters, he or she charges a fee to the dog's owner. The fee varies according to the handler's expertise and reputation, and ranges anywhere from $25 per dog per show to $75 for most handlers. Very experienced and successful handlers charge as much as $110 per dog per show. They also charge bonus fees for special placements they might receive. Handlers winning a Group First may charge the dog's owner a bonus fee of anywhere from $50 to $250.

Very successful professional handlers have been known to make yearly salaries in the six-figure range.

DOG TRAINER

Believe it or not, dogs are not born knowing how to behave—they must be taught! While instincts govern a dog's actions with other dogs, humans must carefully cultivate a dog's behavior around people.

The job of teaching a dog how to act properly in human society belongs to the dog trainer, a professional who works directly with both dogs and people. Dog trainers are experts at communicating with dogs and showing them what is expected of them. Trainers are also adept at dealing with dog owners, who must be taught how to communicate with their own dogs.

Dog trainers work with clients in a variety of ways: They give private, one-on-one training sessions to both dogs and dogs and owners, and often teach obedience and other training classes to groups.

Usually self-employed, dog trainers work out of their own facilities, out of a dog-training center, or in people's homes. Some dog trainers are employed on staff at larger training centers, and receive a salary rather than a per-dog fee.

WHAT DOG TRAINERS DO

The duties of a professional dog trainer often include

- individual training sessions with clients' dogs

- individual training sessions with clients and dogs together

- teaching obedience, agility, and other dog classes

- consulting with clients over the telephone

- visiting potential clients' homes

- evaluating dogs with behavior problems

About the Profession

- Dog trainers are not required to be licensed or certified.
- The National Association of Dog Obedience Instructors (NADOI) and the Association of Pet Dog Trainers (APDT) are two professional organizations representing dog trainers.
- Dog trainers work with individual dog owners, police dog organizations, service dog organizations, rescue associations, and other groups that need dogs trained for specialized behaviors.

WHAT THE JOB IS *REALLY* LIKE

Dog trainers can find themselves working in a variety of conditions, depending on the type of business they have. Some trainers work out of dog training facilities, which are usually busy places where dogs and people are constantly coming and going. Other trainers spend much of their time driving from home to home working with clients' dogs. Still others work in animal shelters or other places where dogs needing training can typically be found.

Because most dog trainers are also small business owners, they can spend a considerable amount of time inside an office returning phone calls and maintaining records.

On occasion, dog trainers find themselves in somewhat hazardous situations when dealing with aggressive dogs. All dog trainers—and particular those who specialize in problem behaviors—are at risk for getting bitten at some point in their careers.

Dog training is a popular field and can be a competitive business. Trainers often have to actively promote their services to ensure that they receive a share of the marketplace.

WHY BECOME A DOG TRAINER?

The rewards of being a dog trainer can be great:

- the satisfaction of knowing you are helping to improve the lives of dogs and their owners

- the chance to work with dogs on a daily basis

- the opportunity to meet and interact with different people

- the ability to own your own business

TRAITS YOU'LL NEED

- a deep love of dogs

- a desire to work with people as well as dogs

- understanding and knowledge of canine behavior

- skills at teaching both dogs and humans

- a great deal of patience when dealing with both people and animals

- willingness to continue learning

- good business know-how

TRAINING AND CERTIFICATION

There are several ways to learn the expertise of dog training. The first is to attend a dog training school, which will teach you the basic skills you need to know to begin apprenticing as a trainer. In most cases, you will need a high school diploma or GED to apply to a dog training school.

Another way to learn dog training is to study under an established trainer, working as an assistant. Volunteering at local animal shelters and for canine community groups will help you hone the skills you learn on the job. You should also read as much as you can about dog training, take seminars on the subject, and do all you can to learn on your own.

No government licensing or certification of dog trainers currently exists, although the Association of Pet Dog Trainers (APDT) currently offers training videos, book lists, a newsletter, and conferences with seminars on training. The National Association of Dog Obedience Instructors (NADOI) offers official endorsements to member trainers. To become a NADOI member, you must have at least five years' experience in obedience training and have taught at least 104 class hours over a minimum of two years as a full-charge instructor.

EARNINGS

Dog trainers who have done their homework and are qualified to train dogs can begin charging around $10 an hour for their work. As their experience and reputation grows, this amount can increase to whatever the competition in the area will allow. Trainers who own their own businesses and are successful can earn as much as $60,000 per year or more.

A Person
Who's Done It

MEET CAROL BYRNES

VITAL STATISTICS

Carol Byrnes and her husband, Dana, own Diamonds in the Ruff, a dog training school in Spokane, Washington. Carol got her first taste of what it was like to be a dog trainer after successfully working with a problem dog while she was in high school. She now describes her job as something she truly loves.

Life on the Job

Q: *How long have you been working as a dog trainer?*
A: I trained my first dog in 1974 and taught my first class as a club volunteer in 1978.

Q: *What did you do prior to this career?*
A: Out of high school, I worked at a retirement home dining room (I learned a lot about dealing with people there!) and later got a job

cleaning cages and working the front desk of a local humane society.

Q: What made you decide to become a dog trainer?

A: I had always loved animals and did horse 4-H and taught our childhood dogs all sorts of tricks over the years. But it was a very tough little Blue Heeler who hated other dogs and was suspicious of people she didn't know that led me to enroll in obedience classes. I spent a lot of time coming early before class and staying after class with a fabulous instructor who graciously spent the extra time I needed to help me turn her into a well-trained dog. That is where I learned firsthand that training a dog isn't a mechanical skill, but is more about building a relationship between dog and owner. I think that and seeing how training saved this puppy from truly becoming a dangerous adult was my inspiration and what compelled me to attend more and more classes and decide that I wanted to eventually be able to help other dog owners train their own dogs.

Q: What kind of education and training did you receive for this career?

A: My initial training was working as a volunteer assisting and eventually instructing for a local dog obedience club. As a club member, I worked long hours with no compensation, worked on the training committee and acting as the assistant director of training, creating curriculum, writing handouts, and training other instructors, learning by doing.

Once bitten by the bug (but never by a dog), I traveled many miles and spent a lot of money attending hundreds of training seminars and training camps to learn about dogs from the inside out, from the best in the business, in all facets of training and behavior modification. I studied animal behavior and learned about the science of training. I bought, borrowed, and read books and more books, watched videos, and trained and showed several of my own dogs over many years. I then took a very long, detailed essay test to become endorsed by the National Association of Obedience Instructors, and joined the Association of Pet Dog Trainers.

Q: How did you get your first job?
A: A friend of mine whom I knew from the training club opened her own dog training school and asked me to teach for her. My husband and I taught there for four years before opening our own school.

Q: What are some of the training jobs you have had?
A: In 1978 I started as a volunteer trainer for an obedience club, and still do it. I also worked with many dogs and people over many years at the local humane society, where I learned a lot about dog behavior and handling stressed animals and educating less-than-responsible owners.

I also did volunteer work with Doberman Pinscher rescue and later Greyhound Pets Rescue, fostering and placing many dogs over several years. Much of fostering requires retraining and rehabilitation of dogs that have not had good beginnings, and teaching new owners how to help their dogs adjust to their new homes.

My husband and I opened our school in 1996, where we teach classes all year. We have five contract instructors and five assistants working with us.

Q: What do you like most about your job?
A: I get paid to do what I love.

Q: What do you like least about it?
A: It is a 24-hour-a-day, 7-day-a-week job. And since I work at home, I never get to "go home from work." I also spend so much time teaching everyone else to train their dogs that I find it difficult to make the time to train my own!

Q: What qualities do you believe a person needs in order to be successful as a dog trainer?

A: Patience, energy, the ability to admit that there will always be more to learn, a love of animals, and most of all, a love of dealing with people.

Q: What advice would you give to people considering dog training as a profession?

A: Do it because you love it, not because you want to make a lot of money! Most of your pay comes in the satisfaction of knowing you are providing a service, and in doing what you love, not a big bank account. Be willing to pay your dues, do plenty of volunteer work, and be in the right place at the right time.

BOARDING KENNEL MANAGER

Once upon a time, the family dog had nearly constant companionship at home. Someone was always in the house (usually Mom), and when the family went on vacation once a year, they either took the dog or left him with a friend or neighbor.

But in today's more hectic world, dogs have a lot more to cope with. People go away more often than once a year—in fact, in homes where both spouses work and travel for business, dogs are often without their family members around for days or weeks at a time.

Probably as a result of this change in our lifestyle and also our more protective attitudes toward our pets, the business of boarding kennels has been on the rise. While pets used to be left in the care of a neighbor during an overnight absence, longer time away from home along with wanting to make sure the pet has the best possible care has changed owner needs.

Someone has to run the facilities that house dogs and cats while their owners are away, and this is where the boarding kennel managers come in. Kennel managers oversee the day-to-day operations of a boarding facility, managing kennel staff and ensuring that the pets in their charge are well cared for.

In most cases, the kennel manager is also the owner of the facility. In some situations, the manager is employed by whomever owns the boarding kennel. Either way, the duties for this position are similar, although kennel owner-managers have more responsibility since with them, "the buck stops here."

WHAT BOARDING KENNEL MANAGER DO

Boarding kennel manager duties include

- managing kennel staff and making sure that pets are fed, exercised, kept clean, and generally cared for

- hiring (and firing) staff as needed

- interacting with customers

- assisting with the care of the animals, including exotics such as birds and reptiles, in some cases

- marketing and promoting the kennel

- managing budgets and payroll

- bookkeeping

About the Profession

- Boarding kennel managers can be either self-employed or work for an outside-owned kennel.
- Approximately 8,500 boarding kennels are in operation in the United States.

- The majority of pets kept at boarding kennels are dogs.
- The American Boarding Kennel Association represents the boarding kennel trade in the United States and offers kennel accreditation.
- Kennel managers are also employed by animal shelters, veterinarians, grooming shops, and government agencies.

WHAT THE JOB IS *REALLY* LIKE

Boarding kennel managers work around dogs all day long, which means coping with plenty of noise, namely barking. Managers also spend some of their time outdoors, but the majority of their time is spent monitoring kennel help and doing office work.

Dealing with the public is also a big part of the job of a boarding kennel manager. Customers with questions and complaints are often the responsibility of the person who is managing the facility.

Just as with the management of any business, boarding kennel managers are responsible for maintaining the bottom line. Considerable pressure can come with this, especially during slow periods involving weather or economic climate.

WHY BECOME A BOARDING KENNEL MANAGER?

- the chance to work around pets, primarily dogs

- the ability to provide pets with good care while their owners are away

- the chance to own your own business

- the possibility of earning a good salary

TRAITS YOU'LL NEED

- a strong affinity for both dogs and cats

- a desire to provide pets with good care

- supervisory experience

- business management skills

- good communication and customer service skills

TRAINING AND CERTIFICATION

To get a job as a boarding kennel manager—or to start your own boarding kennel—you need to have a high school education and preferably more. Courses on running a small business can be extremely helpful, as can classes on animal care and science.

Hands-on experience caring for animals is also necessary before taking on this job; in order to ensure that the animals at your kennel are being properly cared for, you need to know at least the basics of animal husbandry.

You can receive accreditation as an individual from the American Boarding Kennels Association. Certification programs are available at three levels: pet care technician, advanced pet care technician, and certified kennel operator. The organization also provides accreditation to boarding kennels that meet the group's nearly 200 standards.

EARNINGS

Boarding kennel operators employed by privately owned facilities can make anywhere from $25,000 to $40,000, depending on where the facility is located and the amount of responsibility in the position. Managers who own their own kennels can earn a salary in the range of $50,000 to $300,000, depending on the size and success of the business.

PET-SITTER

Not too long ago, when pet owners went on vacation, they simply asked the next-door neighbor to feed the cat or walk the dog while they were away. These days, with lifestyles being as hectic as they are, pet owners have turned to professional pet watchers—more commonly known as pet-sitters—to take care of their pets in their own home while they are away on vacation, business trips, or at work during the day.

People who pet-sit for a living do most of their work in other people's houses, traveling from place to place. They care primarily for dogs and cats, but also count small animals, reptiles, birds, and even livestock among their charges. They clean up after these pets, feed them, exercise them, and provide them with companionship in their owners' absence.

Pet-sitters are self-employed and responsible for doing their own advertising. Once established, many pet-sitters take on clients only through word of mouth.

WHAT PET-SITTERS DO

The duties of the pet-sitter include:

- feeding and watering a variety of animal pets including birds and reptiles

- cleaning cages and yards of pet waste

- walking dogs

- playing with and petting animals

- administering regular medications to pets

- evaluating pets' general health

- taking pets to the veterinarian for emergency care if warranted

- watering plants, taking in the mail, and retrieving the newspaper

About the Profession

- Approximately 90 percent of pet-sitting businesses are owned by women. The remaining 10 percent are owned by men, and men and women partners (5 percent each).
- California has the most pet-sitters of any state.
- Pet Sitters International, the National Association of Professional Pet Sitters, and Pet Sitting Associates, LLC, are three professional organizations representing pet-sitters.

WORKING CONDITIONS

Pet-sitters spend most of their time in other people's homes. The type of animals the pet-sitter cares for the most often will determine how much time is spent indoors versus outdoors. Pet-sitters who do a lot of dog walking and who also care for horses and livestock spend the majority of their time outside—regardless of the weather, incidentally.

Traveling is also part of the job of pet-sitting. Pet-sitters who work at the job full time spend a considerable amount of their day driving from one home to the next to care for the animals.

Because animals need care at all times of the day, pet-sitters often work odd hours; they rise early in the morning and sometimes don't finish until late at night.

WHY BECOME A PET-SITTER?

If you love animals, pet-sitting can be a very rewarding career because of the following:

- the chance to spend most of your working time caring for animals

- the opportunity to work outdoors

- the knowledge that you are providing pets with companionship during their owners' absence

- the ability to set your own hours

- the freedom to live anywhere you choose

TRAITS YOU'LL NEED

- a love of animals

- experience caring for different kinds of pets

- good people skills

- responsibility and self-motivation

- a desire to work for yourself

- access to a car

TRAINING AND CERTIFICATION

You don't need any formal education to be a pet-sitter, although you must have experience caring for animals. It can also be helpful to take a certificate program in animal science through a trade or correspondence school to help boost your knowledge of animal care.

Since pet-sitters are essentially small-business owners, it's important to have some know-how when it comes to running a business. This information can be gleaned by taking a continuing education course or two in small-business management.

Pet Sitters International also has a voluntary training and accreditation program that allows its members to achieve pet-sitting accreditation at four levels: pet-sitting technician, advanced pet-sitting technician, master pet-sitting professional, and accredited pet-sitting service. The programs take anywhere from one month to two years to complete, depending on the level of accreditation.

INCOME POTENTIAL

The amount of money a pet-sitter makes a year depends on how much time the person devotes to his or her business.

Pet-sitters are paid by the visit. The average fee is $12 to $15 for a 30-minute visit. For homes where more than one pet must be cared for, some pet-sitters charge an extra $3 per dog and $2 per cat. Special services such as dog walking often warrant an extra fee of $8 to $24 an hour.

Pet-sitters who work full time in urban areas can earn as much as $40,000 per year.

A Person
Who's Done It

MEET DANIELLE WILLIS

VITAL STATISTICS

Rhode Islander Danielle Willis has always loved animals and has a particular affinity for horses. After working in both barns and kennels, she decided to start her own business taking care of other people's pets. Since 1997 Danni has been pet-sitting on a regular basis for a variety of creatures, including snakes, turtles, dogs, cats—and, of course, horses.

Life on the Job

Q: *What did you do for a living prior to becoming a pet-sitter?*
A: I worked with developmentally disabled adults in a group home and day program setting.

Q: *What made you decide to become a pet-sitter?*
A: I have always loved animals and knew from the time I was little that I wanted a job with horses or dogs. I began horseback riding at age 11 and was hooked. I have worked at many barns and kennels

in my area. One day a woman asked the barn owners if she knew of anyone who could take care of her animals while she went on vacation. My name came up and that was my first pet-sitting job. It took me two years after that job to decide that pet-sitting was something I really wanted to do. I love my job and all the animals that I get to meet.

Q: What kind of education and training did you receive for this career?
A: I have over 15 years' experience with horses and house pets. I never went to college to learn what I know about animal care; everything I learned was hands-on training.

Q: How did you get your first job?
A: All my first jobs were through word of mouth; in fact to this day, I hardly advertise at all.

Q: What kind of clients do you usually work for? What are some of their pets?
A: Most of my clients are vacationers. Some pet-sitters make all their money doing daily dog walks but I really don't want to only pet-sit 12 to 15 hours a day. Most of my clients require an early morning visit, an after-work visit, and a late night one. I enjoy this because I have the rest of my day to do other things that interest me.

I currently have one client who uses me three days a week, every week. This client lives on a farm with 9 dogs, 16 turtles, and one cat. He is my most interesting and reliable client.

To my knowledge, I am the only professional pet-sitter in my area with such extensive horse experience. I have one client with a breeding farm. I have had to handle her stallion, broodmares, and foals. Horses are my favorite clients. But mostly I care for dogs and cats. Sometimes I care for rodents and fish and birds. Presently, I have a 3-foot-long Colombian red tail boa constrictor vacationing in my living room. He is extremely friendly and a joy to care for.

Q: *Do you ride the horses that you pet-sit?*
A: No, I do not ride my clients' horses. I wouldn't even if they asked because I am not a horse trainer and I also do not like to ride alone in case anything were to happen. The horses I care for get turned out into pastures during the day so they can play and run and pretty much exercise themselves.

Q: *What do you like most about your job?*
A: I love to get paid to play with animals. And my mother said I'd never make a living at this kind of work!

Q: *What do you like least about it?*
A: I don't really enjoy putting in 12 to 15 hours of work in a day but when you have a horse addiction to feed (my own), you must go to work. Not every day is that hectic but when you also factor in that I have another job modeling at a local art school, the days can get very long.

Q: *Please describe a typical workday for you.*
A: On a day that I only pet-sit, I usually get up between 6:00 A.M. and 7:00 A.M. to walk dogs or feed cats or muck out stalls. Sometimes I stay at my clients' homes so it's easy to just roll out of bed and let their dogs out or whatever. Depending on the number of clients, my morning rounds are done any time between 10:00 A.M. and 11:00 A.M., then it's off to the barn or to run errands. If it's a barn day, I drive 45 minutes each way to see my horses. Then around 4:00 P.M. I start my after-work rounds. Usually that takes till about 7:00 P.M. and then I go home to eat and relax a little before the late night rounds. There are many nights that I stumble into the house and go right to bed at 11:00 or 12:00 P.M., only to be up in six

hours to do it all again. On days that I model, that whole schedule gets pushed around to accommodate four to seven hours of modeling. That makes for a long day!

Q: *What advice would you give to people considering pet-sitting as a profession?*

A: You have to really love animals, of course, but you also have to have good people skills. The owners are the ones who are hiring and paying you. If they don't feel good about their first impression of you, they are not going to hand over the keys to their homes to you. Always be courteous, honest, and professional. Check out a professional organization like the one I belong to, Pet-sitters International. See if you can work as an independent contractor for another pet-sitter to see if you like the work before opening your own business—but let the other pet-sitter know this up front.

VETERINARY TECHNICIAN/ASSISTANT

One of the most prestigious jobs with animals that does not require a college degree is that of veterinary technician or assistant. Veterinary technicians and assistants work alongside veterinarians in animal clinics, caring for small animals and exotic pets such as birds and reptiles. Technicians are also employed at zoos and laboratories, helping veterinarians in a variety of capacities related to animal health.

The most common setting for veterinary technicians and assistants is a small-animal clinic that caters to pets. Depending on the clinic, the jobs of veterinary technician and assistant may have the same duties or completely different job descriptions. In some animal clinics, veterinary assistants do everything from assisting in surgery and taking blood to answering phones. In other hospitals, veterinary assistants spend most of their time at the front desk, dealing with clients, answering the phone, and keeping records for the clinic while the technicians do the majority of hands-on work with animals.

WHAT VETERINARY TECHNICIANS/ASSISTANTS DO

Veterinary assistants whose primary job is office work will be expected to:

- maintain client records on the computer

- set up appointments

- greet clients

- answer phones

- order supplies

They may also be asked to perform some of the duties expected of veterinary technicians.

Most veterinary technicians spend the majority of their time working directly with animals. They work closely with the veterinarians at the clinic, and are directly responsible for the care of many of the animals interned at the hospital.

Some of the duties of veterinary technicians include:

- assisting with surgery, including monitoring of animals' heart and respiratory rates

- helping veterinarians with exams

- drawing blood, giving injections, and performing other routine procedures

- cleaning cages, exam rooms, and operating rooms

- feeding and medicating admitted pets

- monitoring admitted pets

Veterinary technicians are also employed by laboratories and zoos.
Technicians who work in laboratories are responsible for providing food
and water to a variety of different animals, including dogs, cats, rats, mice,
rabbits, and livestock. Their duties include:

- cleaning cages

- monitoring animals and evaluating their condition

- administering medications

- preparing laboratory samples for examination

- sterilizing equipment

- recording information on research being conducted

Veterinary technicians who work for zoos assist veterinarians in caring
for sick or injured zoo animals. They also assist veterinarians with breeding
programs and other special projects.

About the Profession

- Around 45,000 veterinary assistants and technicians are
  employed in the United States.
- Forty-one states currently have certification programs for veterinary technicians; four of these are voluntary.
- More than 75 veterinary technology programs are accredited by
  the American Veterinary Medical Association (AVMA).
- Jobs for veterinary technicians and assistants are expected to
  increase within the next decade.

WHAT THE JOB IS *REALLY* LIKE

Life for veterinary technicians and assistants who work in animal clinics can be fast and furious. Patients are constantly coming and going, the phone is always ringing, surgeries need to be performed, and animals need to be fed and medicated. The many duties of the job keep veterinary technicians and assistants extremely busy during their shifts.

The pace in laboratories is somewhat more subdued, although the more animals housed there, the more work the veterinary technicians will have in one day. Zoos are similar to veterinary clinics in that a large number of animals need care on a daily basis, making things hectic for technicians responsible for these creatures.

Because animals need veterinary care 7 days a week, nearly 24 hours a day, veterinary technicians and assistants are expected to work on weekends and at odd hours of the day and night. Holidays are also workdays for many technicians.

Aside from the fast pace of animal clinics, veterinary technicians and assistants are also exposed to considerable emotional stress. Sick, injured, and dying animals are a part of daily life for people in these jobs. For technicians who work in laboratories and have strong feelings about animals, the reality of animal testing and research can be difficult to endure.

Even though the job is stressful and the hours are long, the pay for veterinary technicians and assistants is surprisingly low, so low, in fact, that many technicians and assistants find it very difficult to support themselves only on what they make at this job.

WHY BECOME A VETERINARY TECHNICIAN/ASSISTANT?

Though the job is challenging and the pay low, veterinary technicians and assistants find significant rewards:

- the chance to work closely with dogs, cats, birds, reptiles, and other animals

- the ability to help sick and injured animals

- involvement in the exciting world of veterinary medicine

TRAITS YOU'LL NEED

- concern and compassion for animals

- a strong interest in and aptitude for veterinary medicine

- tolerance for a high-stress environment

- the ability to work within a team

- good people skills for dealing with clients

- the ability to follow instructions

TRAINING AND CERTIFICATION

Veterinary assistants who plan to work at the front desk of an animal clinic, maintaining patient information files on the computer, and dealing with clients and telephone appointments need a high school diploma or GED. Computer skills are helpful, along with some knowledge of animal science, which can be learned by taking courses or studying under the tutelage of a veterinarian.

Veterinary technicians who will be working closely with animals and alongside veterinarians require more education, as well as state veterinary board accreditation in most states, before they can practice.

Some veterinary technicians obtain a bachelors degree in veterinary technology, biology, or animal science to prepare themselves for a career as a veterinary technician, but this level of higher education is not required; a two-year education in an American Veterinary Medication Association (AVMA)-accredited junior college or trade school program is all that is needed to pass state accreditation exams. Veterinary technicians who graduate from these programs receive either a certificate, a diploma, or an associate degree. After completing one of these programs, graduates are eligible to take the state veterinary credentialing examination.

Several correspondence courses are also available for veterinary technicians, although the AVMA does not accredit such courses. Instead, the AVMA recommends that prospective veterinary technicians learn the skills needed for the job at an accredited school that uses live animals in a teaching environment.

EARNINGS

Veterinary technicians don't make as much money as one might think, given their skills, level of education, and need for accreditation. Pay typically starts at $8 an hour, and rarely goes above $13 an hour, even for experienced technicians.

Veterinary assistants who do only office work start at slightly above minimum wage. With good management skills, veterinary assistants can eventually become clinic managers, with a subsequent increase in pay.

A Person Who's Done It

MEET MELISSA REIS

VITAL STATISTICS

Californian Melissa Reis began working for a veterinarian right out of high school. Starting out as a kennel assistant, she gradually advanced to veterinary technician, a job in which she works with many types of animals, performs all kinds of tasks, and that she has found to be extremely rewarding.

Life on the Job

Q: *What made you decide to become a veterinary assistant?*

A: Growing up I had always wanted to be a veterinarian. I had a strong love for animals and ultimately felt that a career as a veterinary assistant would be something that would help me fulfill my dreams of helping and learning about all kinds of new animals.

Q: *What kind of training did you receive for this career?*

A: Right after high school, I took a veterinary assisting class at a local adult education school to see if this career was the right one for me. I took a one-semester course and loved every minute of it. I received a certificate in veterinary assisting and found that it was something that came very naturally to me.

Q: *How did you get your first job as a veterinary assistant?*
A: After getting my certificate, I immediately went job hunting. Over the course of a week, I filled out applications at almost every veterinary hospital in the area. I was so sure that with my certificate I would immediately be hired. What I learned months later is that book smart is not always what they are looking for; hands-on experience is what is really wanted. Finally, I received a phone call from the head technician at a local clinic asking me if I wanted a job as a kennel assistant.

Q: *What has been your work history as a veterinary assistant?*
A: I worked as a kennel assistant first, then moved up to veterinary assistant at the first clinic that hired me. I then went to work at another clinic as a veterinary assistant and progressed to veterinary technician in a year. I moved on to yet another animal hospital, and worked there for six years. In that time, I went from veterinary technician to receptionist to office manager. I am now capable of performing any task in a veterinary hospital, from cleaning cages to surgery to billing.

Q: *What do you like most about your job?*
A: I enjoy working with all kinds of animals, helping them when in need. I also like practicing preventive medicine so clients' pets can live longer, healthier lives.

Q: *What do you like least about your job?*
A: A few things: the fact that money is involved in treating pets and that clients often won't want to spend it. Long, stressful days, and seeing animals die.

Q: What advice would you give to people who are interested in becoming veterinary assistants or technicians?
A: Volunteer at a busy hospital first to make sure you can handle the stress. If you can, this can be a most rewarding job.

A FEW KEY POINTS TO REMEMBER

• It's important to have hands-on experience with dogs, cats, and other pets before pursuing a career with these animals.

• Most jobs dealing with pets call for good physical health, including a lack of allergies to animal dander.

• Pay is often low in jobs dealing with pets; be certain you are willing and able to live on a minimal salary in exchange for working with animals.

CHAPTER FOUR

Jobs with Horses

Horses are beautiful and amazing creatures that have inspired humans throughout the ages. Some people are truly addicted to horses and will do just about anything to spend time with them. If this sounds like you, you may be a good candidate for a career in the equine industry.

WORKING WITH EQUINES

The good news for people who love horses but don't plan to go to college is that there are an abundance of horse-related careers out there that do not require a college education. They do, however, require considerable experience handling horses, as well as physical strength and good health.

The type of horse-related job you choose will depend on what interests you most. Do you prefer to handle horses on the ground rather than ride them? Or is being on the back of a steed a sensation you love more than anything else? Do you have a burning desire to combine your love of horses with a passion for teaching? Or do you have a strong sense of business acumen you would like to put to use in the horse world? Your answers to these and other questions will help you determine which area of the horse world seems best suited for you.

In this chapter, we'll look at several horse-related careers that require little or no formal schooling. However, while you may not need to attend a university and come out with a specialized degree, you will need to have plenty of knowledge of the horse world, horse husbandry, and equine behavior to succeed in any of these fields. This means you should spend considerable time getting to know horses and learning all about them before even attempting to follow one of these career paths.

EQUINE MASSAGE THERAPIST

While many jobs relating to horses have been in existence for hundreds of years, the job of equine massage therapist is a relatively new one. A spin-off of sorts from human massage therapy, equine massage therapy is conducted by specially trained massage therapists who work directly on horses. Their goal is to use massage to relax muscle spasms, relieve tension, and enhance muscle tone. They also strive to increase circulation and range of motion in the horse.

Equine massage therapists are generally self-employed and travel from client to client. Some also provide massage therapy for other animals besides horses (including humans), but most focus exclusively on horses. In some cases, equine massage therapists work in conjunction with a veterinarian, although many equine veterinarians have not completely embraced equine massage therapy as a legitimate form of healing.

WHAT EQUINE MASSAGE THERAPISTS DO

The duties of the equine massage therapist include:

- evaluating a horse's condition by examining the horse and questioning the owner

- determining whether the problem would be best helped by massage therapy or another approach

- assisting the owner in rectifying whatever has caused the problem, if appropriate

- providing massage therapy to the horse

About the Profession

- Equine massage therapy is a relatively new field and is still growing.
- Equine massage therapy is a nonregulated profession, and there is no national test or certification procedure.
- A number of schools offering training in equine massage therapy exist around the country.
- Equine massage therapy is most popular in the Far West, mid-Atlantic, and Pacific Northwest regions of the United States.
- Owners of horses used for dressage or racing are most likely to use the services of equine massage therapists.
- The majority of equine massage therapists work at this career part time.

WHAT THE JOB IS *REALLY* LIKE

Equine massage therapists work primarily outdoors, attending to equine clients. They must work in all kinds of weather and conditions. Blowing dust, high heat, extreme cold, and biting bugs are all part of the equine massage therapist's working environment, depending on the time of year.

Equine massage therapists are usually self-employed and spend considerable amounts of time on the road, driving from one client to another. They also work unusual hours to accommodate the schedules of their clients.

WHY BECOME AN EQUINE MASSAGE THERAPIST?

Those who practice equine massage therapy enjoy:

- being able to work directly with horses

- being able to help horses in pain to feel better

- working as their own boss

- spending time outdoors

TRAITS YOU'LL NEED

- a strong affinity for horses

- commitment to undergo formal training in massage therapy

- knowledge of equine anatomy and behavior

- self-motivation

- good communications skills

- willingness to travel to see clients

- good physical health

TRAINING AND CERTIFICATION

No national certification currently exists for equine massage therapists. However, a number of schools offer courses leading to certificates and diplomas in the subject.

Since there is no standardization in the study of this field, it's important to carefully choose the place in which you will study and the method by which you will study. While short three-day or one-week courses may be tempting, longer, more intensive programs are required to teach the proper methods of massage that will truly help horses in need. Becoming a certified massage therapist for humans before enrolling in an equine massage therapy program will increase your skills with horses and broaden your client base.

The International Association of Equine Sports Massage Therapists approves certain certification programs, and is a good source for school recommendations.

An organization called TTEAM Training International also provides training and certification in its own type of equine massage, developed by respected trainer Linda Tellington-Jones. While this type of massage differs significantly from standard equine sports massage therapy in that it is geared primarily toward resolving behavioral problems in horses, it is nonetheless well respected in the equine industry, and also includes various aspects of training.

EARNINGS

Since most massage therapists are self-employed, their income varies depending on how many clients they serve. The charge per session is anywhere from $35 to $150, depending on the skill and reputation of the therapist. Of course, the more clients a therapist sees in a day, the greater his or her income.

Experienced equine massage therapists who have been in business for at least 10 years and are well respected can typically make anywhere from $40,000 to $55,000 a year.

A Person
Who's Done It

MEET CELESTE M. RYFA, LMT

VITAL STATISTICS

Celeste Ryfa had a respected position with the United States Equestrian Team (USET) Public and Media Relations office when she decided to switch from her office job to equine massage therapy. She has been working as an equine massage therapist in Rhode Island for the past three years, and has found her true vocation.

Life on the Job

Q: What made you decide to become an equine massage therapist?

A: I've always loved horses and wanted to work with them. Although the promotion of equine sports events is important, I felt a desire to work more closely with the horses themselves. One day I came upon an article about equine sports massage therapy. Having had to deal with my own low back pain, which massage therapy gave the most relief to, I thought it would be a perfect blend of my passion for working with horses, and helping them live better, healthier lives.

Q: *What kind of education and training did you receive for this career?*
A: I was told that in order to do this field justice and to be the absolute best I could be with the most value for the horses, I really should become a Licensed Massage Therapist (LMT) by attending an approved massage therapy school and work in the field. Then I could attend the Jack Meagher Institute of Muscular Kinetics and Equine Sportsmassage (JMI). Only LMTs can attend this school. So I went to Albuquerque, New Mexico, to attend the New Mexico School of Natural Therapeutics. Because this school was full time, a 750-hour course of study, we were in session for six full months and encouraged to work on as many people outside of school as we could. Shortly after I returned home, I took the Foundation level course at JMI, and the following year took the Intermediate level course and have been working in the field ever since with a human, canine, and equine practice.

Q: *What was your first equine massage therapy job?*
A: The first horse I ever worked on was a referral from JMI. She was an Arabian mare at a Western barn. It was the middle of winter and cold, but the first time I worked her, my first horse client, I was euphoric for days afterwards. Since then, I have worked on Thoroughbred racehorses, competitive dressage, show jumping and eventing horses, Western and gaited horses, hunters, and retirees. I have been kicked at, stared at, and ignored. I've also been thanked profusely by the horses when the knot that's been driving them crazy melts away. There's nothing like it in the world!

Q: *What are your days like?*

A: Between keeping appointments for humans as well as dogs and horses things can get pretty crazy. I have an office for humans to go to, but I am on the road a lot doing home and barn calls for the animals. Some days I have to work on all three; other days are just people days or just dog days or just horse days or sometimes just a mix of two out of three. I can start by 8:00 A.M. and work until 7:00 or 8:00 P.M. or work 3:00 to 6:00 P.M. or 9:00 to 11:00 P.M., 1:00 to 5:30 P.M., and so on. I have to be very organized and very good at following directions. And I have to buy good footwear!

There are always phone calls to return and appointments to make and cancellations to take, not to mention eating, running errands, and taking care of my own dogs. If you like routine, don't get into this business.

Q: *What do you like most about your job?*

A: I like getting my hands on horses, working closely and personally with them. I love being outdoors and definitely love to see the difference in the animals during and after the session. They are so honest and show results so quickly. I love knowing that with a little bit of help from my hands they feel better and can go out and do the job that is asked of them more comfortably and easily. Human beings ask a lot of their animals and I love knowing I can help give a little something back. I love having a mixed human and animal practice; I'll never get bored or burned out.

Q: *What do you like least about it?*

A: I hate the flies, the humidity, and the freezing, but on the whole it is better than being in an office all the time. I hate the frustration I feel when some people don't understand the benefits or the reasons behind sports massage therapy for horses. No matter how much explaining is done, they see this only as a form of frivolous pampering of pets.

Q: *What would you say are your most important duties?*
A: Aside from helping the horses, it's educating people about the value of massage therapy. If no one understands the importance of massage for the animals—the benefits, the reasons for it, when and when not to get it done, the importance of working with the veterinarian, the farrier, the saddler, and the trainer—then no one will use massage.

Q: *What advice would you give to people considering equine massage therapy as a career?*
A: Think long and hard about it. It is difficult but fulfilling work, and it takes time to establish a reputation and a clientele. You should enjoy being your own boss, be organized, and love horses. And don't think you'll become independently wealthy doing this.

Also, become a human massage therapist first. Until you know what muscles feel like, until you learn to feel the differences in them, the releases, the adhesions, the attachments, the anatomy, then you aren't doing justice to yourself or the horses you work on. It takes lots of time and practice to learn human massage therapy; horse massage therapy should come from all that learning and practice. Even if you do not want to continue in practice on people, the skills and lessons learned on them in school are invaluable.

If you love horses, don't mind hard work, or getting dirty, this can be one of the most rewarding professions you may ever find.

FARRIER

Most people have heard the expression "No hoof, no horse." These four words are more than just a saying—they are gospel truth. Without healthy feet, horses can't walk, trot, or run; often, they can't even stand. Horses with sickly feet suffer tremendously, since equines were designed by nature to spend nearly 75 percent of their lives standing up. A horse that can't stand or walk is a horse not long for this world.

This is where the farrier comes in. Also known as a shoer or blacksmith, farriers are responsible for caring for a horse's feet. The skill of the farrier determines whether or not a horse is capable of standing, walking, and being ridden. A good farrier keeps his clients' horses feet in good condition, and plays a big part in keeping the horse healthy and the owner happy.

WHAT FARRIERS DO

Farriers have several different duties relating to horses' feet:

- trimming the nail of the hoof. The nail on a horse's hoof grows continuously and must be trimmed every six to eight weeks, depending on the horse.

- fitting and applying shoes to the horse's hooves. Farriers work with steel and fire, and use tools such as rasps, nails, hoof trimmers, and hammers.

- correcting abnormalities of the foot and soundness problems by using different methods of trimming and shoeing. Farriers often consult with equine veterinarians during this process.

About the Profession

- Three different organizations represent farriers in the United States: the American Farriers Association, the Guild of Professional Farriers, and the Brotherhood of Working Farriers Association.
- According to the *American Farriers Journal*, there are an estimated 50,000 to 70,000 farriers in the United States.

- About 92 percent of American Farriers Association members are male; 8 percent are female.
- Schools all around the country offer training for farriers, who can earn certificate degrees in farrier work, or associate or bachelor's degrees in equine science with a specialty in horseshoeing.

WHAT THE JOB IS *REALLY* LIKE

Farriers typically work out of the back of a pickup truck or out of a small trailer. They work in all kinds of weather—heat and cold, rain and wind. They travel many miles each week to see their equine clients, who are often scattered around a somewhat vast geographical area. Farrier work requires a lot of bending and stooping and general physical strength. It also calls for considerable experience handling horses, and can sometimes be hazardous since not all horses are cooperative when their feet are being handled.

WHY BECOME A FARRIER?

Those who make a living in the profession of horseshoeing find the rewards tremendous. These rewards include:

- being able to work outdoors instead of in an office

- working hands-on with horses

- feeling the gratification of helping a horse that is suffering from foot problems

- meeting horse owners and talking to them about their horses

- the flexibility and many rewards of running your own business

TRAITS YOU'LL NEED

- physical soundness—you'll be performing hard physical labor in often unpleasant weather conditions

- a love of horses and understanding of their behavior

- good business sense

- an ability to deal with people such as owners, trainers, and veterinarians

- a detail-oriented mind

- willingness to risk personal safety when working around horses

TRAINING AND CERTIFICATION

Because farrier work is a combination of both art and science, considerable training is required. It's vital that you know exactly what you are doing before you start working on a horse's feet. Just as a skilled farrier can do wonders for an ailing horse, a poor farrier can permanently destroy a horse's soundness.

To become certified with the American Farriers Association (AFA), you must be able to pass written and hands-on examinations. Before you can do this, you must have received formal training at a farrier school or learned on the job as an apprentice to an experienced farrier.

Most farrier school programs are six to eight weeks in duration, and will prepare you to take the basic AFA Intern Classification certification test. With this classification, you can begin working on horses while under the supervision of a certified farrier.

To apply for basic certification with the AFA, you must have worked as a farrier for at least one year. After two years as a farrier, you may apply for Journeyman Certified Farrier status. Both certifications require tests to determine your skill as a farrier.

The Brotherhood of Working Farriers Association (BWFA) also offers certification for farriers, at apprentice, journeyman, and Master Farrier levels, with requirements similar to that of the American Farriers Association.

EARNINGS

Farriers first starting out in their profession can expect to earn in the area of $15,000 to $25,000 a year. After working full time for 10 years and building up a clientele, skilled farriers can make as much as $75,000 a year, depending on how much work they choose to do. The majority of farriers in the United States make between $40,000 to $79,999 a year.

Keep in mind that farriers are small-business owners, and thus have the expenses associated with running their own company. You'll need a pick-up truck in good working order, a small trailer, a forge (a furnace for working metal), and farrier tools and equipment.

GROOM

Have you ever gone to the racetrack and wondered who took care of the horses both before and after the race, and how?

The people responsible for the daily care of racehorses, breeding stallions, pregnant and foaling mares, and even expensive show horses are often grooms, whose job it is to care for everyday equine needs.

WHAT GROOMS DO

Grooms spend a considerable amount of time with horses—nearly every moment of their day, in fact—and are involved in just about every aspect of their care, including:

- feeding and providing water

- hand walking and riding

- observing horses for signs of illness

- administering medication

- bathing and brushing

- cleaning stalls, paddocks, barns, and breezeways

- cleaning and repairing saddles and bridles

- loading horses into trailers

- performing repair work around the stable

Grooms are usually employed by large racing stables, breeding barns, show barns, and boarding stables.

About the Profession

- The larger the facility and the more expensive the equine inhabitants, the more jobs are available for grooms.
- Some grooms work in exchange for housing or riding lessons.
- Grooms can specialize in areas such as handling racehorses or breeding animals.

WHAT THE JOB IS *REALLY* LIKE

Grooms often find themselves working in inclement weather, since horses must be cared for whether it's hot, rainy, or snowing. They often work long hours and on the weekends as well, sometimes traveling with their equine charges to races and sales away from home.

The work of a groom is very physical and requires him or her to be in good health and prime shape. Grooms must also have a considerable amount of equine knowledge and experience around horses to be successful—and safe—in their career. Most grooms not only need to know how to expertly handle horses from the ground, but must also know how to ride well.

WHY BECOME A GROOM?

People who work as grooms enjoy the following advantages to the job:

- the ability to be with horses virtually all the time

- varied duties that require both physical work and mental alertness

- being able to work outdoors instead of in an office

- the chance to see horses they have cared for go on to big wins or great show ring successes

TRAITS YOU'LL NEED

- physical hardiness and a willingness to get dirty

- love and knowledge of horses

- an ability to deal with horse owners, trainers, and other grooms

- willingness to risk personal safety when working around horses

- a driver's license and willingness to learn to drive farm equipment

TRAINING

One of the best things about becoming a groom is that no formal training is required. Prospective employers look for individuals with considerable experience working with horses, however, whether your own horse or others'. They also want to see good riding ability since many grooms are expected to ride the horses they care for in order to exercise them. It is therefore important that you gain as much experience as you can working with and riding horses if you want to become a groom.

EARNINGS

One of the downsides to being a groom is the pay. Grooms rarely make more than $25,000 a year, tops, and that is after considerable years in the business. The entry-level salary is usually as low as $12,000 a year. The good news is that free housing is often provided to grooms, so this is one less cost they have to incur on their small salaries.

JOCKEY

Probably the most high-profile job in the horse world is that of the jockey. Nearly everyone has seen jockeys at work, leaning forward atop galloping horses racing for the finish line. It's a glamorous line of work but a dangerous one, and not something that everyone is cut out for.

The primary responsibility of the jockey is to ride his or her client's horse to the finish line—and win. In order to achieve that goal, the jockey must work with the horse's trainer and owner. Jockeys are involved with the training of the horses they ride, and are part of the team that works to create a successful racehorse.

Jockeys work at different career levels, and will have different duties according to the level of racehorses they ride. Famous riders such as Angel Cordero, Jr. and Chris McCarron are at the upper echelons of the profession and ride top Thoroughbred horses; the majority of jockeys ride horses that compete at lower stakes. These horses not only include Thoroughbreds running in smaller races, but also other breeds used for racing such as Quarter Horses, Appaloosas, and Arabians.

Most jockeys use the services of a jockey's agent, an individual who helps them procure mounts in exchange for a portion of the jockey's fee.

WHAT JOCKEYS DO

The responsibilities of the average jockey include:

• riding horses in races

• working with trainers to aid in the horses' performance

- riding racehorses during training and exercise sessions

- helping with care and maintenance of racehorses, depending on the level of the jockey

Jockeys typically work on a freelance basis and are hired by horse owners or trainers. In order to make a living, a jockey must work for a number of clients. Also, because a horse can run faster when carrying a lightweight rider, jockeys must be small in stature to be guaranteed work.

About the Profession

- Jockeys can find employment riding different racehorse breeds, including Thoroughbreds, Quarter Horses, Arabians, and Appaloosas.
- The majority of jockeys are male.
- The career of jockey is considered a dangerous profession.

WHAT THE JOB IS *REALLY* LIKE

The life of the jockey is a difficult one because of the dangers involved, the hectic schedule, and the pressures of having to find mounts and win. In order to be successful as a jockey, one must start at a young age, often while still completing high school. Also, because work as a jockey is so strenuous, most jockeys retire earlier than individuals in other less arduous animal-related jobs.

Jockeys spend a lot of time around horses, mostly sitting on their backs. Most of the jockey's riding time is not spent during the race, however. Jockeys must mount up in the paddock area and walk or trot the horse to the starting gate. This takes longer than the actual race, which is rarely more than a couple of minutes in length. They also ride horses in training sessions.

Because horse races are held all over the world, jockeys spend a lot of time traveling. Depending on the success of the jockey, travel accommodations can be anywhere from luxurious (a deluxe hotel) to downright uncomfortable (the back of a van).

The typical 9-to-5 schedule experienced by office workers is alien to the jockey. Irregular hours and weekend work are typical for this line of work. Most jockeys must be early risers too, especially if they exercise and help train their clients' horses.

Horse races are held in all kinds of weather, and jockeys must be willing to ride in the heat, the rain, and the wind. They must also be willing to risk their lives for their profession, as riding racehorses is a dangerous way to make a living. A serious spill during a race can result in debilitating injury or even death.

WHY BECOME A JOCKEY?

If you love being on the back of a galloping horse, there can be no greater thrill than riding a racehorse. Jockeys experience that thrill on a regular basis as they sit astride the fastest horses in the would.

Other benefits to being a jockey include:

- being able to work outdoors around horses

- working on a freelance basis and being your own boss

- the opportunity to see different parts of the country

- having a job that helps you stay in good physical shape

- the excitement of being on a winning team when your horse wins a race

TRAITS YOU'LL NEED

- a diminutive stature

- courage and the willingness to expose yourself to physical danger

- exceptional skills as a rider

- a strong sense of competitiveness

- good health and athleticism

- a sense of fearlessness and readiness to take risks

- a firm understanding of horse behavior and care

- the ability to work under pressure

- good communication skills

- self-discipline

- a sense of teamwork

- knowledge of the rules, tactics, and procedures of horseracing

- a willingness to travel

TRAINING

Most jockeys start out as exercise riders, riding horses during training hours, and then become apprentice jockeys. Apprentice jockeys typically work with horse trainers and learn the nuances of horseracing. To become an apprentice jockey, you must be at least 16 years old.

Finding a mentor jockey or trainer to help you learn the profession is the best way to develop your skills and make the contacts you need.

EARNINGS

Exercise riders start with a salary of about $400 a week. In order to gain experience and visibility riding in races, young jockeys often forgo their exercise rider salaries in exchange for the chance to ride in a race. For this reason, salaries tend to decrease temporarily after an exercise rider has made his or her move to become a working jockey.

Once a jockey has enough mounts to make a living, he or she can earn as much as $25,000 to $30,000 a year, depending on the state.

A successful young jockey can make as much as $75,000 a year. The top earners make salaries well into the six-figure range.

A Person Who's Done It

MEET DONALD MILLER, JR.

VITAL STATISTICS

The son of a jockey, Donnie Miller started riding in races at the age of 17 and pursued his job with fervor. During his 16-year career, he became Maryland's top jockey and won the 1983 Preakness Stakes, the second leg of the famed Triple Crown, on a horse named Deputed Testamony.

Life on the Job

Q: *What did you do prior to becoming a jockey?*

A: Homework! I was still in school. The high school I was attending had a program for students that allowed us to take mandatory courses during half a day and work the other half. Naturally, I needed the permission of my parents. One of several things I found interesting was that students were not allowed to take two English courses in one semester. Consequently, I completed one of those English credits during summer school in order to graduate early.

Also, this program was originally designed for students with family hardship. It's a good thing I had graduated early; I was able to make it to the top of the jockey standings before I went to my graduation ceremony. I would never have had the time to finish school and do it right.

Q: *What made you decide to become a jockey?*
A: My dad was a jockey from 1958 to 1963, just before I was born. He knew racing was a tough life—seven days a week and not much pay. I was not even allowed around racehorses until I was close to 12 or so. Dad felt there was no way his kids were going to ever have to work as hard as he did; they were going to graduate from high school and go to college if it killed him! By the time I was allowed around horses, he had a string of about 15 horses, in training. He had cheap, willing labor in my brother and sisters and me during the summer months—well, at least me anyway. Everyone in my family was small. I thought, "My dad can teach me how to ride; he has about 15 horses in training. I'm small, what else is there?" Bottom line: I wanted to be just like my dad—he was my idol.

Q: *What kind of education and training did you receive for this career?*
A: Most all education and training to be a jockey comes from the "school of hard knocks" as there is no formal jockey school in the United States. The basics were taught to me by my dad. He showed me how he did things, how others might do it, and to always find what works best for me because everyone is different. I learned to be an astute observer of others and learn what worked for them. I wasn't afraid to ask questions or to even borrow a technique from someone much more accomplished then I.

Q: How did you get your first job?

A: My first job was working for my dad; I didn't really have much choice. Actually I didn't really even want another choice. Having my dad in the business certainly helped, but there have been far more successful jockeys then I who had no one to guide them early, so that shouldn't stop anyone.

Q: How did you go from being a starting rider to winning a leg of the 1983 Triple Crown?

A: Once I had established myself as the number one jockey in Maryland early in my career, my agent and I continued to grind out a grueling schedule of riding races six days a week and many times going to neighboring states to ride races at night. I was able to finish the first year as the top young rider (apprentice) in races won in the United States in 1981. We were able to parlay that success with a lot of hard work into national rankings for the next couple of years. I had an opportunity to ride Deputed Testamony as a two-year-old several times. The jockey who had been riding him as he got older chose to ride another horse in the Preakness that year. None of the "big name" jockeys could or would make arrangements to ride him in the Preakness because he was a long shot to win. Because I had been the top jockey in Maryland for over two years at that time with daily experience riding over the Pimlico track, it was decided to give the local guy a shot. The rest is in the history books.

Q: What did you like most about your job?

A: Without a doubt I loved the competition. The funny thing was that the competition was me. My entire goal in riding races was to get my horse from the starting gate to the finish line as fast as the law of physics would allow him to go. Naturally I wanted to win, but by focusing on the things I could control, everything else didn't really matter. If I didn't bring out the best in my horse, I didn't do my job. Although I did get a huge kick out of trying to outsmart the other jockeys, that's generally not what wins races.

Q: *What did you like least about it?*
A: "Making weight." Every day, like most jockeys I had to walk into the jockeys' room and step on that *scale*. It was like someone standing there with a sledge hammer, waiting to say "You were very, very bad last night."

Q: *What was a typical workday like for you?*
A: Throughout my career but especially early, my agent and I would get to the track between 5:30 and 6:30 A.M. to visit the three racetrack stable areas that were in Maryland to talk to the people who trained the horses. My agent spent countless hours trying to convince the trainers that they just had to have "his jockey" on their horse. I spent my time exercising the horses for speed workouts as a favor in the hopes that I would get to ride the horse in a race. About 9:30 A.M. I would then head to the jockeys' room to face that horrible monster—the scale. If I had enough time I would take a quick nap, then go to the steam room to sweat off the extra water weight that I had gained back the night before. Post time for the first race is usually 12:30 or 1:00 P.M. Races run about every half-hour and I would normally ride at least seven races and most times nine to ten a day. Once the races are over, I get to have a normal life like everyone else—sometimes.

Q: *What advice would you give to people who are considering becoming a jockey?*
A: However you make your way to the track, ask a lot of questions, find out who is willing to help young jockeys and not take advantage of your inexperience. Probably the best people to talk to are the jockeys themselves; most will bend over backwards to point you in the right direction because the more you learn, the safer they will

be when you're out there riding side by side with some of the greatest athletes in the world.

And above all, be ready for a career that is very unpredictable, extremely dangerous, and very rewarding.

TRAINER

For those who love working with horses, one of the most rewarding careers to have is that of horse trainer. Horse trainers spend most of their time working directly with horses, teaching them everything from the basics of being handled by humans to the intricacies of racing or upper-level dressage.

Horse trainers come in many different forms. A good number of trainers work with racehorses, including Thoroughbreds, Standardbreds, Quarter Horses, Arabians, and Appaloosas. Others train show horses in any one of a number of different disciplines, such as open Western, three-day eventing, or driving. Still others train horses for recreational riding or special activities such as therapeutic riding.

The majority of horse trainers are self-employed, although some work exclusively for particular show or racing barns. Those who are self-employed own their own facility, or pay a commission to the owner of the facility where they work. Most trainers have a number of different clients, and specialize in a particular type of training.

WHAT TRAINERS DO

Trainers have different duties, depending on the type of training they do and whether or not they have one or more assistants to help them. Some duties include:

- basic horse care, which can include feeding, grooming, and cleaning stalls. (Trainers who have assistants usually don't have to do this type of work.)

- medical care. Many trainers are responsible for providing medical care to horses in their charge. While a veterinarian will diagnose and prescribe treatment, it is often up to the trainer to administer the treatment to the client's horse.

- groundwork. Most trainers will work directly with horses "on the ground," meaning that they do some of their training without riding the horse. This can include teaching the horse to lead, lunge, drive with side reins, or stand for examination, depending on the trainer's specialty.

- saddle work. With the exception of most racehorse trainers, the majority of trainers ride the horses they are training, both for schooling and in competition.

About the Profession

- Thoroughbred racehorse trainers are represented by a member association, the United Thoroughbred Trainers of America.
- Individuals wishing to pursue a career as a racehorse trainer have the unusual option of learning the profession on the job, obtaining a certificate through an accelerated program, or receiving a four-year college degree in the subject.
- Trainers of pleasure and show horses often also function as riding instructors, teaching horse owners how to ride their horses after the trainer has trained them.

WHAT THE JOB IS *REALLY* LIKE

Because horse trainers work directly with horses, they spend most of their time outdoors except in the most inclement of weather. While snow and torrential downpours usually limit the amount of work a trainer can do with a horse, heat and cold do not stop the trainer from getting the job done.

Horse trainers often find themselves working long hours, starting early in the morning and ending in the evening. They also sometimes work seven days a week, depending on the type of training they do and the number of clients they have. The work tends to be year-round, but busiest during show and racing seasons.

Travel is another aspect to most horse trainers' lives. Trainers who work with show horses and racehorses must travel to shows and meets. Only the top trainers can afford luxury conditions when traveling—the majority stay in campers or inexpensive hotels.

WHY BECOME A TRAINER?

If you really love horses and the outdoors, you stand to reap many rewards from being a horse trainer, including:

- the chance to work directly with horses on a daily basis

- the knowledge that you are helping a horse meet its greatest potential

- the chance to teach horse owners how to better enjoy and ride their horses

- the opportunity to meet and bond with fellow horse lovers

- the rewards of being your own boss (for trainers who are self-employed)

TRAITS YOU'LL NEED

- a talent for riding and working around horses

- good health and athleticism

- a love of horses and a strong understanding of their behavior

- good business sense if you plan to be self-employed

- the ability to deal with people (remember, your clients are humans, not horses!)

- teaching skills that can be applied to both horse and human

- a willingness to risk personal safety when working around horses

TRAINING AND CERTIFICATION

If you want to become a horse trainer, you need to learn as much about horses as you possibly can. This means becoming an excellent rider, studying equine behavior, and learning all about horse care.

Most certificate and diploma programs for trainers at private colleges require a high school diploma or GED, and some equine experience beforehand. To gain horse experience before enrolling in such a program, spend as much time as you can around horses. Getting a job on weekends at a local stable mucking stalls, and taking riding lessons on a regular basis will give you the background you need to get started. Many racehorse trainers start out as grooms and even exercise riders.

Certificate programs in horsemanship and horse training are available from private learning institutions, and can provide an excellent foundation for would-be horse trainers, particularly those who want to train show horses. Established trainers are always looking for assistants who are knowledgeable about horses and willing to learn more. Working as an assistant trainer is an excellent way to get on-the-job training and help with job placement.

If you prefer to become a show or pleasure horse trainer without any formal education, start working as a groom or assistant for an established trainer. You will be able to learn a lot as you work alongside the trainer, and will most likely be able to train on your own in time.

Non-racehorse trainers do not need a license or certification; however, the British Horse Society, which certifies trainers in England, has approved some educational facilities in the United States for certification of horse trainers. Having BHS certification will make you more marketable as a trainer.

If your goal is to train racehorses, you must start out as a groom or "hot walker," and work your way up to assistant trainer, then trainer. To work as an assistant trainer, working at a racetrack or for a private racing barn, you'll need to pass an assistant trainers' examination and be issued a license. Each state has its own racing board that licenses trainers, and rules differ from state to state. In most states, the assistant trainers' examination consists of written, oral, and practical portions.

After working as an assistant trainer, you can eventually move up to trainer provided you pass the state examination for the licensing of trainers.

EARNINGS

Assistant trainers starting out can expect to make $10,000 to $14,000 a year. Depending on the type of training and the number of clients, established trainers working for at least 10 years can make as much as $45,000 a year. Top show and racehorse trainers make anywhere from $75,000 to $100,000 a year.

RIDING INSTRUCTOR

Unlike horse trainers who teach mostly horses, riding instructors teach only humans. Riding instructors give lessons to riders—often beginners—and teach them not only how to ride a horse, but also the nuances of horsemanship and all that it entails. Sometimes, trainers and riding instructors are one and the same person.

Riding instructors usually specialize in one particular discipline. English (hunt seat), Western, and dressage are three disciplines that are often taught by riding instructors. Some instructors teach only beginners; others teach riders at high levels of experience, depending on their own expertise.

Riding instructors tend to be self-employed people who set up shop at a local riding stable. In some cases, the stable will actually employ the instructor, but this is not the norm. Typically, the instructor is responsible for bringing in his or her own clientele, paying a commission to the stable owner, and providing the horses that are used in lessons. In some cases, instructors teach students to ride on the student's own horse.

WHAT RIDING INSTRUCTORS DO

The duties of the riding instructor include:

- teaching beginners how to groom, saddle, and bridle horses

- helping beginners and/or experienced riders master a particular riding discipline

- caring for horses owned or leased by the instructor for lessons

- marketing his or her services

- maintaining business and accounting records, if self-employed

About the Profession

- Riding instructors are not required to be licensed or certified in the United States.
- Most instructors tend to specialize in teaching either children or adults.
- The majority of riding instructors are female.

WHAT THE JOB IS *REALLY* LIKE

Riding instructors spend the majority of their time outdoors in often unpleasant weather. While few people will take lessons during a downpour or snowstorm, it's not uncommon for riding lessons to be given during the heat of the summer or on very chilly winter days. When weather is particularly bad, lessons might be cancelled, but lesson horses still need to be cared for.

The primary workplace of the riding instructor is the riding stable, and all the dust, flies, and odors that come with it. If you have an uncontrolled allergy to hay, horses, or dust, a career as a riding instructor is definitely not for you.

Weekends are popular times for riding lessons, so most instructors spend their Saturdays and Sundays at the stable, teaching others to ride. Lessons are also given early in the morning on weekdays and in the evenings, after school and work is over for most people.

WHY BECOME A RIDING INSTRUCTOR?

Definite benefits come along with the profession of riding instructor, such as:

- the ability to spend nearly all of your work time in the company of horses

- the chance to work outdoors

- the opportunity to be your own boss

- the satisfaction of helping others improve their riding skills

- the chance to meet people from all walks of life

TRAITS YOU'LL NEED

- good physical health, as much of your time will be spent standing and walking and sometimes riding as you teach

- an ability to communicate with both humans and horses

- a willingness to work independently

- strong skills as a rider in your chosen discipline

- the ability to evaluate the riding skills of students and help each progress to the next level

- the ability to motivate students

TRAINING AND CERTIFICATION

In the United States, riding instructors are not required by law to be licensed or certified; however, several organizations offer voluntary certification programs: the American Riding Instructors Association (ARIA), American Association for Horsemanship Safety, Inc. (AAHS), Certified Horsemanship Association (CHA), United States Dressage Federation (USDF), and the North American Riding for the Handicapped Association (NARHA). Being certified by one or more of these organizations will not only help increase your likelihood of gaining clients or employment, but it will also help you become a better instructor.

The American Riding Instructors Association offers the American Riding Instructor Certification Program, which identifies skilled riding instructors. In order to pass the test for certification in either combined training, distance riding, dressage, driving, hunt seat, open jumping, recreational riding, saddle seat, sidesaddle, or stock seat, you must be able to pass a series of tests meant to evaluate your knowledge and professionalism.

Recognition from the American Association for Horsemanship Safety Inc., comes in the form of a safety certification. After completing a 40-hour intensive training program, riding instructors take a mounted test that proves they can ride safely and adequately. They must also prove their ability to perform CPR and first aid. Levels of certification include Safety-Certified Riding Instructor (ability to teach basics of horsemanship correctly to beginner through advanced riders), Safety-Certified Riding Instructor—Basic (ability to teach basics of horsemanship correctly to beginner and intermediate riders), and Safety-Certified Assistant Riding Instructor (must be at least 18 years old and teaching under the direct supervision of a Safety-Certified Riding Instructor).

Certification from the Certified Horseman's Association requires evaluation in five different areas:

1. safety
2. equine knowledge and ability
3. teaching
4. group control
5. responsibility and professionalism.

To be certified, riding instructors attend a five- to seven-day certification clinic. A minimum of four practice lessons, a riding evaluation, a written test, and participation in workshops on risk management, teaching techniques, professionalism, and herd management are all included. At the end of the clinic, certification is given to those who pass.

The United States Dressage Federation certifies riding instructors who teach the discipline of dressage. The organization offers certification in two categories: Training through Second Level, and Third through Fourth Level Certification. A series of educational courses is offered by the USDF to help instructors get the knowledge they need to gain certification. Candidates are tested on six sections: Riding, Lungeing Horse, Lungeing Horse/Rider, Teaching, Verbal, and Written Exam. Candidates must pass all six sections for certification.

The North American Riding for the Handicapped Association offers instructor certification status in three levels for therapeutic riding instructors: registered, advanced, and master. To become an NARHA certified instructor, you must gain some experience working with individuals who are using riding to help overcome a handicap. You can do this by volunteering at an NARHA Operating Center in your area. You can also attend an NARHA-Approved Training Course.

In addition to any of these voluntary certification programs, you can also learn to become a riding instructor by taking a certificate or diploma program in riding instruction at a private school that offers an equestrian program. These schools usually require a high school diploma or GED, along with some prior experience working with horses.

Working as a groom or assistant to a riding instructor is another way to learn the ropes, although you most likely won't be paid for your work. Some instructors will exchange lessons for the work of assistants and grooms, however.

EARNINGS

The salaries earned by riding instructors vary widely, depending on the amount of hours spent teaching, the type of instruction given, and level of teaching experience. Part-time instructors can earn anywhere from a few hundred dollars a year to $6,000 or $7,000. After 10 years of teaching full time,

$15,000 to $25,000 is common. Top instructors can earn as much as $75,000.

EQUINE FACILITY MANAGER

Whether it's a racing barn, a breeding facility, or a boarding stable, every equine establishment needs a manager—someone who runs the day-to-day operation and makes sure everything goes smoothly. This person is the equine facility manager.

WHAT EQUINE FACILITY MANAGERS DO

Facility managers are salaried employees of whomever owns the stable or barn being managed. Duties often vary depending on what kind of operation he or she is managing, and may include:

- dealing with horse owners and trainers on a daily basis

- bookkeeping for the facility

- maintaining records on the horses kept at the facility

- assisting with hands-on care and/or breeding of horses

- making sure all aspects of the facility are in proper working order

- marketing for the facility

- supervising facility personnel

- operating farm machinery

About the Profession

- The majority of equine facility managers have both equine and business management experience.
- Many equine facility managers previously worked in another area of the horse industry prior to managing a horse facility.
- Some equine facility managers will work for a reduced salary in exchange for boarding services for their own horses.
- Smaller facilities tend to employ managers on a part-time basis.

WHAT THE JOB IS *REALLY* LIKE

Equine facilities managers are fortunate to be able to work outdoors much of the time and be around horses. They often have to deal with unpleasant weather, as do all people in outdoor jobs, and spend a lot of time working around dust and flies at various times of the year.

Equine facility managers typically work out of an office that is located on the grounds of the facility, but don't typically spend most of their time in it. The job's various duties keep the facility manager moving around the stable, whether it's caring for horses, repairing broken fences, dragging an arena, or supervising feed deliveries.

The managers of equine facilities typically work on the weekends and several days a week, and start out early in the morning. Hours can be long, stretching well into the evening.

WHY BECOME A FACILITIES MANAGER?

The best reasons to become the manager of an equine facility include

- being able to work outdoors

- working independently

- spending time around horses

- being in a position of authority

- meeting different people

- being physically active

TRAITS YOU'LL NEED

- a deep affinity for horses

- thorough knowledge of equine behavior and care

- keen attention to details

- good communication skills and the ability to get along with people

- good business acumen

- proficiency in marketing, bookkeeping, and computer skills

- ability to handle farm equipment and make minor repairs on fences, stalls, etc.

- physical stamina and strength

TRAINING AND CERTIFICATION

A number of specialty colleges offer certificate and diploma programs for those wishing to get started in equine facility management. These programs are usually accelerated, and focus exclusively on handling horses and managing a horse-related business.

Taking extension courses in bookkeeping, business management, and equine care or veterinary sciences can help prepare you for a career as an equine facilities manager. You should also consider working as a groom, training assistant, or stable worker with the goal of eventually moving up to stable management. The more experience you have working around horses and managing them, the better your chances of landing a job in this field.

A high school diploma or GED is usually required for a position as an equine facilities manager, and is required by most schools offering certificate or diploma programs in stable management.

EARNINGS

The salary you make as an equine facilities manager depends on what part of the country you work in and what type of facility you are managing. Managers who run large breeding operations can make upwards of $50,000 a year. Those who manage small boarding facilities full time rarely make more than $30,000. Part-time managers can earn anywhere from $7,000 to $10,000. Keep in mind that many equine facilities provide housing to managers, which helps cut down on living expenses.

A Person
Who's Done It

MEET SUZIE HALL

VITAL STATISTICS

Suzie Hall had grown up around horses, and knew that somehow, some way, she would end up working with them. After trying her hand at training, Suzie settled on a career managing boarding stables. Her job not only allows her to be around horses, but also to manage their care and welfare.

Life on the Job

Q: *How long have you been working as a boarding stable manager?*

A: I've been working one year as a manager, and three years in assistant manager positions. Right now I'm the manager of El Toro Stables in Irvine, California. Before that, I worked as an assistant at stables in Medford and Portland, Oregon.

Q: How did you earn a living before becoming a boarding stable manager?

A: I worked for several hunter/jumper trainers around the country. I also owned and operated my own boarding stable in Montgomery, New York. I cleaned my own stalls, and did all my own feeding and upkeep on the property. It was very challenging, especially in the snow, but I loved every minute of it!

Q: What made you decide to become a boarding stable manager?

A: My parents were horse trainers since before I was born so I always thought the love of horses must be in my blood. I didn't feel happy unless I was around horses, so I decided to pursue some kind of work involving them—first, it was training, then eventually running my own boarding stable.

Q: What kind of education and training did you receive for this career?

A: My parents, being trainers, were a big part of my education. I also learned a lot by working with other trainers.

Q: How did you get your first job?

A: I was boarding my horse at a stable when a position for assistant manager opened up. The manager at the time approached me with the offer. He said he thought I'd be good for the job because of my knowledge of horses and my personality.

Q: What kind of personality traits did you have that made you a good candidate for that job?

A: To be a good stable manager, you have to be very personable and easygoing. You also need to be fair, be a good problem solver, and be caring and compassionate.

Q: What is a typical workday for you?

A: At 9:00 A.M. I open up the office and check telephone messages. I then walk through the stables and around the grounds, taking note of anything or any animal that needs attention. At noon, I drag the riding arenas with the tractor, and then do office work after that, which includes making phone calls and ordering supplies.

Q: *What do you like most about your job?*
A: Being around horses and being outside are the best things.

Q: *What do you like least about it?*
A: Dealing with difficult boarders.

Q: *What would you say are your most important duties?*
A: The care of the horses and overall safety.

Q: *What advice would you give to people considering stable management as a career?*
A: Be aware that you will have to deal with lots of different people and personalities. The horses are the easy part!

STABLE WORKER

If you love horses, spending your days taking care of them can be a wonderful job. In various different equine facilities all across the country, stable workers are employed to feed horses, muck out stalls, repair fences, and do a variety of other chores meant to keep horses happy and healthy, and their facilities safe and in good repair.

WHAT STABLE WORKERS DO

Those employed as stable workers typically have the following responsibilities:

- feeding horses two or three times a day

- cleaning stalls, feed bins, and waterers

- dragging arenas to keep footing safe

- repairing fencing and caring for pastures

- blanketing and unblanketing horses

- providing first-aid to horses when needed

- keeping barn aisles and facility areas clean

About the Profession

- Thousands of stable workers are employed throughout the country, and provide the working backbone of the horse industry.
- The majority of stable workers are male.
- Many stable workers live on the property where they work.

WHAT THE JOB IS *REALLY* LIKE

Stable workers must feed and clean up after the horses in their care in all kinds of weather. Whether it's raining or snowing or 100-plus degrees outside, stable workers must still tend to the horses.

For those who work at feeding horses and cleaning up after them, dust and dirt are constant companions. Being a stable worker is a dirty job.

Unlike some jobs that are only Monday through Friday, stable workers often put in six-day weeks. They start their chores early in the day, and work well into the evening, depending on what needs to be done.

The duties of the stable worker entail hard physical labor. With the exception of a couple of breaks a day, stable workers are always on the move. A typical day in the life of a stable worker involves feeding horses, mucking stalls, dragging the arena, repairing equipment, and sweeping barn aisles. In between these major chores, any number of other duties may arise.

WHY BECOME A STABLE WORKER?

For people who love hard work and being around horses, the job of stable worker is a good one. Benefits include:

- working outdoors

- being near horses

- plenty of physical activity

- working with your hands

TRAITS YOU'LL NEED

The job of a stable worker is not easy. To be happy in this position, you must possess:

- a desire to work outdoors

- a penchant for hard physical work

- good health and a strong back

- experience with horses

- the ability to follow instructions

- a willingness to work long hours

TRAINING AND CERTIFICATION

Stable workers need to have experience with horses and some knowledge of carpentry and mechanical repair. No formal training is required. A high school diploma or GED is not necessary.

EARNINGS

Stable workers typically start out earning the minimum hourly wage. After being employed for a period of time, they typically receive slightly higher wages. A few dollars over minimum wage is usually all the stable worker can expect to earn; however, many equine facilities provide housing and even health benefits for stable workers as part of a compensation package.

WRANGLER

Over the past several decades, the popularity of vacation ranches—once known only as "dude ranches"—has skyrocketed. City dwellers long for a week or two out in the country each year, where they can ride a horse and be close to nature.

As a result of the growing popularity of this type of getaway, the need for wranglers to work with horses used at vacation ranches has increased over the past couple of decades. Consequently, more and more opportunities for wranglers are opening up around the country, although competition for the best jobs can be intense.

Wranglers work both seasonally and year-round, and spend the majority of their time outdoors in spectacular countryside, tending to horses and socializing with each other and ranch guests. Although the hours are long and the work is hard, most wranglers wouldn't trade their jobs for anything in the world.

WHAT WRANGLERS DO

The wrangler's primary job is to care for the horses on a vacation ranch, and aid the guests with their riding. The duties ascribed to most wranglers include:

- feeding and grooming horses

- saddling and packing horses for trail rides

- taking guests on trail rides or cattle drives

- providing riding instruction to guests

- repairing and cleaning tack

- mending fences and ranch equipment

- participating in guest socials such as dances and hayrides

About the Profession

- Many wranglers start in the profession early, often right out of high school.
- The majority of wranglers are male.
- Some wranglers find employment on working cattle ranches that do not provide guest services.

WHAT THE JOB IS *REALLY* LIKE

Wranglers spend the great majority of their time outdoors working with horses, and sometimes cattle. Beautiful scenery in some of the country's most pristine wilderness areas provides the setting for the wrangler's tasks.

Since ranch vacation guests prefer to ride in pleasant weather, wranglers do most of their work when the weather is nice. However, even when weather prevents guests from riding out on the trail, horses still need to be cared for—and this is the wrangler's job.

Many wrangling jobs are seasonal. The busiest times for guest ranches are late fall through mid-spring in warmer areas of the country, and late spring to mid-fall in colder areas. Because of this, wranglers often work and live in different places half of the year.

Hard physical work and long hours are the name of the game for wranglers, who have to get up early to feed the horses and then stay up late participating in guest activities such as dances, talent contests, and other events.

No matter how tired they might be, wranglers are expected to remain cheerful and pleasant to guests throughout the day and evening.

WHY BECOME A WRANGLER?

If you love horses, people, and the outdoors, there are some very good reasons to become a wrangler:

- spending most of your work time riding and caring for horses

- working outdoors in beautiful wilderness settings

- meeting and getting to know people from around the world

- working with your hands

TRAITS YOU'LL NEED

- excellent riding and horse-handling skills

- stamina and the willingness to work long hours

- strength and good physical health

- good communication skills and a friendly personality

- a love of the outdoors

- flexibility in your lifestyle and a backup job, as many wrangling jobs are seasonal

TRAINING AND CERTIFICATION

Although no formal training is required to be a wrangler, vacation ranches typically hire wranglers with at least a high school diploma or GED who like people and have strong skills with horses.

Some outfits will hire trainees with little or no horse experience for summer jobs, sometimes without pay. This is a good way to learn the ropes and develop an "in" with a particular vacation ranch.

EARNINGS

Wranglers don't make a lot of money. Minimum wage or just above it is typical for wranglers first starting out; however, room and board, along with a share of tips, is standard for most wrangling jobs.

Many wranglers start out as trainees and work their way to the top to become head wrangler, where they can earn $20,000 or so a year, depending on the vacation ranch and how much time during the year the wrangler works. Some wranglers ultimately end up starting or purchasing their own vacation ranches, changing careers from wranglers to outfitters.

A Person
Who's Done It

MEET CLEVE KIDD

VITAL STATISTICS

Canadian Cleve Kidd grew up in the province of Ontario and rode horses on his parents' farm, but it wasn't until he started working for his cousin at a vacation ranch in British Columbia during summer breaks from school that he realized what he wanted to be—a wrangler.

Life on the Job

Q: *How long have you been working as a wrangler?*
A: Five years. I started when I was 14, working in the summer. I'm now a wrangler at Anchor D Guiding & Outfitting Ltd. in Black Diamond, Alberta, located in the Canadian Rockies.

Q: *What did you do before becoming a wrangler?*
A: I was going to high school and working with my dad during the fall and winter months as a machine operator at a mold injection plant in Ontario.

Q: *What made you decide to become a wrangler?*
A: My cousin Dewey Matthews is head wrangler at the Anchor D, and talking to him and being around him made me think about getting into this job. It seemed like an interesting career, plus, I saw what he had accomplished, and how it had given him a sense of confidence in everything he does. It also seemed like a great way to meet people from all over the world.

Q: *What kind of education and training did you receive for this career?*
A: I had ridden a little before starting to work as a wrangler in the summer, but I learned most of what I needed to know right on the job. I was taught horsemanship and how to properly saddle and unsaddle horses—I was given a lot of them to do! On pack trips, I was taught to pack properly, and I was shown how to do knots and hitches. I even learned about starting colts and how to work with young horses. Also, since driving big trucks and trailers is an important part of the job because our horses get hauled a lot, I learned how to do this too.

Q: *How did you get your first wrangling job?*
A: Dewey saw that I wanted to work outdoors with horses and suggested I work at the Anchor D during the summer.

Q: *What is a typical work day for you?*
A: I get up at 6:30 A.M. If we are in camp, I feed the horses. If we are on the ranch, I bring the horses in. I then brush and saddle them in preparation for the day's trail ride. I eat breakfast, and then I am ready to hit the trail by 10.00 A.M. I ride with guests for a few hours in the morning, then take them to a lake or a place with a view of the mountains for a lunch stop. We then take a new trail home in the afternoon. Once we get back to camp, I unsaddle the horses, and hobble them. By the time my work is done, it's about 10.00 P.M.

Q: *What do you like most about your job?*
A: Being able to work outside is the best thing. I also enjoy the physical part of it and working with my hands. We raise our own colts to use on the ranch, and I really like riding them too. When you can get a young horse to start responding to your legs and hands, it makes you feel good and gives you a sense of accomplishment.

Q: *What do you like least about it?*
A: The long hours—they can get to you after a while. We try to get one day off a week, but it doesn't always work that way.

Q: *What would you say are your most important duties?*
A: Matching guests with the right horse is a big thing. We also teach the guests to ride as we go along. We will correct them and give them pointers on the trail. The horses do a lot of the teaching, though.

Q: *What advice would you give to people considering wrangling as a career?*
A: If you have an interest in this career, contact an outfitter—a person who owns a dude/vacation ranch. Find someone you can learn from. Some outfitters will take on people who don't know much about horses and train them from scratch. If you do well one summer, you'll be welcomed back the next year.

A FEW KEY POINTS TO REMEMBER

- Get as much experience with horses as you can, even if it means working for free. Just about every horse-related job calls for prior equine experience.

- Evaluate your personality and health to determine if you are comfortable working outdoors in inclement weather and dusty conditions. Most jobs with horses take place in this kind of environment.

- Most jobs with horses don't pay well, especially early in the career. Make sure you have a financial support system in place before you embark on any equine-related career.

CHAPTER FIVE

Jobs with Wildlife

T he definition of *wildlife* is "wild animals and birds," according to *Webster's Dictionary*. Yet when it comes to working with wildlife, the word is extended to mean any species that has not been domesticated.

Those who work with wild animals do so in a variety of settings, including zoos, veterinary hospitals, and of course the great outdoors.

WORKING WITH WILD CREATURES

As we become more and more technologically advanced, our link to nature seems to grow more distant. For most people, life in the big cities means hours spent in an office in front of a computer and less contact with wildlife and the outdoors.

In response to this reality, people are seeking ways to reconnect with nature. Whether it is spending time in wilderness areas observing wildlife, going to zoos to see exotic animals up close and personal, or simply watching fish swim around in a home aquarium, those who want to be in touch with what is still natural in our world are pursuing activities that will help them feel connected to the wildness that is our heritage.

The result of this trend is more jobs concerning wildlife—and an even greater desire among people to get these jobs. While the great majority of these positions call for a college degree, a few do not require it. In this chapter, we'll look at those careers tending to wildlife both in captivity and in the natural environment that require minimal schooling but plenty of practical knowledge.

AQUARIST

Few things are as relaxing as watching fish swim around in a well-designed and well-maintained aquarium. More and more people are discovering this reality and adding both fresh- and saltwater aquariums to their homes and offices.

Someone has to design and care for these aquariums and the fish that inhabit them on a regular basis. While many aquarium owners are adept at doing their own tank design and maintenance, more and more often, people would rather hire someone to do it for them. That is where the job of professional aquarist comes in.

Aquarists are experts who design and maintain fresh- and saltwater aquariums, although saltwater provides by far the most work for those who do this for a living. Some aquarists also specialize in outdoor fish ponds, and do both indoor and outdoor maintenance.

Most aquarists are self-employed and work alone in their business. Other aquarists are employed by small companies that provide design and maintenance as part of their aquarium-oriented services.

WHAT AQUARISTS DO

The duties of a professional aquarist include:

- visiting both residential and commercial clients once or twice a month

- analyzing water and fish health

- changing water, cleaning filters, and removing algae

- treating sick fish

- providing emergency service when needed

- designing aquarium setups from scratch

- consulting with clients on physical design and which fish to purchase

- buying fish and plants from wholesalers

About the Profession

- The majority of in-home aquariums serviced by aquarists are saltwater tanks.
- Most professional aquarists are male.
- The Marine Aquarium Society of North America (MASNA) provides support and education to saltwater aquarists, both amateur and professional, and has regional chapters around the continent.
- No licensing or permitting of aquarists exist other than traditional business licensing.

WHAT THE JOB IS *REALLY* LIKE

Those who work on aquariums for a living spend a great amount of time traveling from one client to another, usually in a van or truck that contains all the equipment they will need to perform the tasks at hand. This means driving in sometimes heavy traffic for those in suburban and urban areas, dealing with bad weather on the road, and being responsible for fuel costs and wear and tear on the vehicle.

Aquarium work can also be physically demanding since it often involves carrying equipment, bending and stooping, and other such activities. Aquarists also spend time interacting with people, talking to clients, and discussing their aquarium needs.

Those who are self-employed must also devote time to marketing and promoting their businesses to ensure a steady flow of clients. Once a business has been established, the majority of work will come from regular clientele. However, it's important to promote the business on a regular basis so new clients will be available when the existing clientele drops off.

WHY BECOME AN AQUARIST?

For those who love keeping aquariums as a hobby, the job of caring for fish and the enclosures they inhabit for a living can provide the following rewards:

- the ability to spend the majority of work time dealing with aquatic life and its habitats

- the chance to work in various home and commercial environments

- the opportunity to meet a variety of people

- the chance to become self employed

TRAITS YOU'LL NEED

- extensive hands-on experience designing and maintaining both freshwater and saltwater aquariums as a hobbyist

- a passion for aquatic life

- the ability to market and promote your own business

- good people skills and the ability to communicate well with customers

- dependability

- a driver's license and access to a vehicle large enough to carry aquarium maintenance equipment

- good physical health

TRAINING AND CERTIFICATION

The great majority of professional aquarists who run their own aquarium maintenance services learned their fishkeeping skills as hobbyists, usually beginning the hobby in childhood. They have attended seminars, read books and magazine articles, belonged to fish clubs, and done everything they possibly could to learn how to design and maintain aquariums for both freshwater and saltwater fish and plants.

In addition to this self-taught knowledge, many self-employed aquarists begin their careers by working for an already established aquarium maintenance service or aquarium store as an employee, eventually starting their own business when they have obtained significant knowledge of fishkeeping.

No certification or licensing is currently given to professional aquarists, although individuals running their own small company must obtain a business license in the county or municipality where they live.

EARNINGS

Aquarists who start out by working for an aquarium maintenance company or aquarium store often begin with a minimum wage salary. Some work on a 50 percent commission for each service call they make. More experienced employees can earn up to $12 an hour.

Aquarists working full time in their own businesses can earn as much as $2,500 a month servicing various clients. This amount usually increases as clients are added to the business and more experience is gained. Salary is based on a $50 to $75 per hour charge—or a monthly labor charge based on these amounts—to clients.

A Person Who's Done It

MEET JOSE SEMPRIT

VITAL STATISTICS

New Jersey resident Jose Semprit has been caring for aquarium fish since he was 11 years old. Seven years ago, he gave up his job as a salesperson at an optical company to follow his heart and become a professional aquarist. Now in business for himself, Jose truly loves what he does.

Life on the Job

Q: *What made you decide to become an aquarist?*
A: After 15 years of being stressed out in my job in the optical field, I felt I needed to change to something more relaxing, something I loved doing. That turned out to be my aquatic hobby.

Q: *What kind of education and training did you receive before starting?*
A: I had the best training one could get: I was an aquatic hobbyist since childhood. I had read books and done a lot of research. I had

also spent time with an aquarium wholesaler, asking questions and helping him in order to learn.

Q: How did you get your first job?

A: I started out working for an aquarium store, where I was doing aquarium service and in-store maintenance. My goal was to learn the business and find out how to set one up for myself. After two years I left to start my own business. Since then, I've built a home-based business designing aquariums and maintaining them. My clients include doctors, a chief executive officer of a company, and working people who enjoy the relaxation of aquariums in their homes.

Q: What do you like most about your job?

A: I like the flexible hours, traveling to different locations, being creative, and doing something I love—plus, it's so relaxing!

Q: What do you like least about it?

A: I am sometimes faced with problems that are difficult to solve. You can do everything by the book and the water tests fine, yet you lose fish. For example, I had a client with a saltwater tank in his family room. Whenever we would add fish to the tank, they would live for a month and then die. This kept happening over and over. Water tests were normal, and biologically, the tank was stable. I couldn't figure out what was going wrong. Finally, I asked him if anyone was smoking near the tank or spraying anything in the room. He said that his wife didn't like the smell that was coming from the tank and so would regularly spray air freshener near it. I suspected that this was poisoning the fish. I asked him to have his wife stop spraying and use extra carbon in the filter to eliminate the odor. Sure enough, that solved the problem. The fish stopped dying.

Q: *What is a typical day like for you on the job?*
A: I get up, have coffee, feed my cat, give her some attention, and go to work, visiting different locations with aquariums needing care. When I do arrive at the place where I'm doing the servicing, I usually test the water first, although I can often tell by eye if the water needs testing. If it's a new client, I test it to give the client peace of mind. I then change a percentage of the water, clean the inside of the tank, refill the water, and do other tasks related to caring for the aquarium.

Q: *What would you say are your most important duties?*
A: Keeping track of my accounts schedule. That means making sure all the aquariums are serviced on time. A happy fish equals a happy customer.

Q: *What advice would you give to people who are considering going into this career?*
A: Make sure the aquarium hobby is something you enjoy and love doing. Also, once you start working, be reliable, truthful, and responsible with your customers.

PARK RANGER

National parks, national forests, and designated wilderness areas are among the most beautiful places in the world. Filled with trees, plants, geological wonders, and of course, wildlife, they represent the jewels of our nation. For many people, being outdoors in these locations is relaxing, refreshing, and even spiritual.

Because the public is appreciating our wild lands even more than it used to—people are consequently spending more time in wilderness areas and national parks—professionals are needed to maintain the integrity of these areas, seeing to it that people obey the rules meant to protect these places, and that all is as it should be on a daily basis.

The profession responsible for much of this wilderness guardianship is the park ranger, an individual whose job it is to protect wild areas, educate and assist the public, and maintain a safe environment for people, plants, and animals. While the job of park ranger is a very competitive one, and those with college degrees have the edge when it comes to getting the jobs, those without degrees but who have significant volunteer experience can and do get hired.

Park rangers are generally employed by the Department of the Interior, working for either the Bureau of Land Management or the National Park Service, two bureaus that fall under Department of the Interior jurisdiction.

While most people enter the profession of park ranger so they can work in a wilderness area, many start their jobs in metropolitan parks located near or within large cities. Rangers who stick with it eventually end up in the wilderness areas they prefer.

WHAT PARK RANGERS DO

The duties of the park ranger can be varied, depending on which bureau the ranger is employed by and what type of work the ranger ultimately chooses after being in the field for some time. For example, generalists do varied jobs, interpretation specialists provide information on wildlife and the environment to the public, law enforcement specialists concentrate on enforcing laws within the parks, and interdisciplinary specialists do a little bit of everything.

Typically, park ranger duties include:

- enforcement of park rules

- answering the public's questions about wildlife and fauna

- patrolling

- working in the visitors' center

- collecting park fees

- giving nature walks and talks to the public

- occasionally handling wild animals (including reptiles) and dealing with wildlife-human problems in the park, such as bears raiding campsites, for example

About the Profession

- Park rangers are employed by government agencies.
- Jobs are extremely competitive and often require waiting for a period of time for an opening to occur.
- Most entry-level positions are found in parks situated near urban areas.
- Housing is often provided to park rangers.

WHAT THE JOB IS *REALLY* LIKE

The working conditions available to park rangers are the number one reason so many people want to get into this career. Park rangers spend the majority of their time outdoors in resplendent settings, surrounded by wildlife and all kinds of natural wonders.

The downside of this is that the weather isn't always agreeable in these very wild places, yet the park ranger must still be outside. Also, in most cases, park rangers are also expected to live in housing provided in or near the area where they will be patrolling, some of which is less than luxurious.

Although park rangers are able to spend time talking about and viewing wildlife, the majority of a ranger's work is spent dealing with other human beings.

Rangers who work in national parks and wilderness areas are often expected to negotiate difficult and dangerous terrain while doing their jobs. The work of a park ranger can also be physically demanding.

Work for park rangers is often seasonal, and few rangers stay year-round on the same job. Some work as rangers only in the summer and have other jobs the rest of the year. They may also be given transfers from one part of the country to another.

Rangers are expected to work weekends and holidays during the busy seasons for wherever they are stationed, and whatever hours are required.

Park rangers specializing in law enforcement must contend with potentially dangerous situations and individuals who are not cooperative. They spend much of their time telling people what they are *not* allowed to do.

Job security is often a problem for park rangers, whose positions are often at the whim of the employing agency, the U.S. Congress, or another bureaucratic entity. When government funds are low, park ranger jobs are often the first to go.

Salaries for park rangers are typically low, although this is offset somewhat by supplied housing.

WHY BECOME A PARK RANGER?

The benefits to this career are many, including:

- a chance to be outdoors in some of the most beautiful places in the country

- an opportunity to be around wildlife

- the chance to educate the public about wild animals

- the knowledge that mangers are helping to protect wild places and their animal inhabitants while helping the public to enjoy them

TRAITS YOU'LL NEED

- a passion for the great outdoors

- a genuine liking for people

- good communication skills

- a thorough understanding of the natural world

- a willingness to live in frugal accommodations

- a readiness to work long and varied hours, and on weekends and holidays

- a willingness to perform a variety of job functions

- tolerance for low pay

TRAINING AND CERTIFICATION

The job market for park rangers is a competitive one, which means that those with college degrees tend to get the majority of the jobs. However, individuals with a high school diploma or GED and significant volunteer experience can bypass the college process and gain entry into the field. At least four years of seasonal volunteer work is needed before a prospective park ranger stands a chance of getting hired. During that time as a volunteer, it's important to foster relationships with others in the field to help ensure employment when the time comes to look for a job.

In addition to volunteer work, courses taken in wildlife biology, forestry, and any other subjects relevant to work as a park ranger can be helpful.

Once employed as park rangers, individuals are sent to "ranger school," which further teaches them what they need to know to do the job as defined by the bureau that employs them.

EARNINGS

Entry-level salaries for park rangers working during the summer only are around $18,000 for those with college educations; those without college degrees often earn a little less. Permanent year-round rangers start at around $20,000 to $30,000, depending on education and experience.

Rangers can advance to management or specialist positions over time and consequently earn higher salaries.

WILDLIFE REHABILITATOR

For people who love wildlife and want to spend most of their time working with wild animals, the job of wildlife rehabilitator is ideal.

Wildlife rehabilitators are experts in the rescue and care of wild creatures. Some rehabilitators work only with birds, others with birds and mammals, other with only mammals, and still others with a variety of different species including reptiles. Some specialize in a particular type of bird or mammal such as hummingbirds or pinnipeds (seals and sea lions).

The job of wildlife rehabilitator involves taking in sick or injured wildlife and caring for it until the animal is well enough to be released back into the wild. Most rehabilitators work with veterinarians who provide assistance on a volunteer or reduced-fee bases. Most wildlife centers don't have the luxury of an on-staff veterinarian, so the rehabilitator takes on much of the job of medicating and treating the animals in the center's care with a veterinarian's guidance.

The great majority of wildlife rehabilitator positions in the United States are on a volunteer basis. However, more paying positions are being created as the skills of rehabilitators are being recognized as valuable, and more funding becomes available for the rehabilitation of wildlife.

Most volunteer and paying jobs can be found in private rehabilitation centers that run on donations. Some facilities also receive financial assistance from local municipalities, and work with animal control agencies to provide veterinary care for wildlife that comes into the possession of animal control agents.

WHAT WILDLIFE REHABILITATORS DO

The typical duties of wildlife rehabilitators include:

- accepting wildlife brought into the facility by the public and by animal control officers

- evaluating the condition of wildlife and determining prognosis and treatment, in most cases, in conjunction with a consulting veterinarian

- providing food and water to animals

- cleaning cages

- administering medication and changing wound dressings

- providing physical therapy and exercise sessions to animals

- answering phones and other office work

- assisting in fund-raising and publicity for the center

About the Profession

- Approximately half of all animals admitted to wildlife rehabilitation centers are successfully released back into the wild.
- In order to possess and care for wildlife, a rehabilitator or facility must obtain a permit from state and federal wildlife agencies.
- The majority of wildlife rehabilitators are volunteers.
- The International Wildlife Rehabilitation Council (IWRC) and National Wildlife Rehabilitators Association (NWRA) are two associations that provide education and support to wildlife rehabilitators.

WHAT THE JOB IS *REALLY* LIKE

Wildlife rehabilitators spend almost all their time working directly with animals. They handle them for exams and treatment, for transport, and to provide them with physical therapy and exercise.

Rehabilitators also have the less glamorous duties of feeding and cleaning up after animals, and therefore they encounter some unpleasant sights and smells (dead mice are a staple of many predatory birds, for example).

Long hours and work on weekends and holidays are typical for wildlife rehabilitators, who must be available whenever animals need them. The frustrations of not enough funding can also be a constant stress for wildlife rehabilitators, who must often work with not enough supplies and other necessities because the money they need isn't available to them.

Wildlife rehabilitators must adhere to strict ethics when it comes to working closely with wildlife in their care. While it may be tempting to bond with the wild animals they are caring for—particularly young ones—doing so will cause the animal to lose its fear of humans, making it less of a candidate for release. It's vital that rehabilitators keep their emotional distance so the animal's ability to return to the wild is not jeopardized.

Stress is a serious component of the wildlife rehabilitator's working conditions, especially when it comes to having to euthanize animals. Statistics show that only about half of the animals admitted to wildlife rehabilitation centers end up being released, meaning that a great many die or must be euthanized. This can be difficult to face on a day-to-day basis.

WHY BECOME A WILDLIFE REHABILITATOR?

A rewarding job, wildlife rehabilitation offers these benefits:

- the knowledge that you are helping wild animals recover from illness and injury and return to the wild

- the chance to spend time working with other people who have the same interest

- the opportunity to assist veterinarians in the treatment of wild animals

TRAITS YOU'LL NEED

- a passion for wild animals

- an interest in veterinary medicine

- knowledge of wild animal biology and behavior

- a willingness to work long hours for little pay

- the ability to deal with the public

- good physical health

TRAINING AND CERTIFICATION

Most wildlife rehabilitators learn their skills on the job while working as volunteers. Most wildlife rehabilitation centers are desperate for volunteers to clean cages and do other mundane chores, so procuring a position as a non-paid worker is easy. This is an excellent way to learn the skills needed to care for wild animals, and could eventually lead to a paying job.

Those serious about wildlife rehabilitation as a career should also take some basic continuing education or college courses in biology, animal science, and conservation as preparation for the job.

The International Wildlife Rehabilitation Council also offers seminars and training classes at wildlife centers nationwide. Some classes are also offered at the organization's annual conference.

Wildlife rehabilitation centers and individuals who care for sick and injured wildlife on their own must obtain permits from state and federal wildlife agencies. Other permits from local agencies may also be necessary.

EARNINGS

The amount of money paid to wildlife rehabilitators varies considerably depending on the particular wildlife center. Some centers can offer only moderate stipends or minimum wage to entry-level rehabilitators, while others can pay experienced rehabilitators as much as $30,000 a year plus benefits. Some centers cannot afford to pay rehabilitators at all, and employ them only on a volunteer basis.

A Person
Who's Done It

MEET KAREN McELMURRY

VITAL STATISTICS

Karen McElmurry is director of The Center for Wildlife in Cape Neddick, Maine. Working as a rehabilitator for the past 12 years, she has found the job to be both challenging and rewarding.

Life on the Job

Q: *What made you want to become a wildlife rehabilitator?*

A: As a child, I had a love of animals and nature. I was the kid who brought home the bird egg that fell from the nest, or the bunny that had been caught by the cat. I knew at a young age that I would work with animals in some way. At 18 I got my first volunteer position at the Michigan Humane Society walking dogs and helping with the cleaning.

Q: What kind of education and training did you receive to become a rehabilitator?

A: All of my experience has come from others in the rehabilitation field. After graduating from high school, I got a job at the Michigan Humane Society where I eventually did some work with wild animals. It was there that I discovered I wanted to work with wild animals and not domestic ones. After leaving that job, I served two internships at other wildlife centers, one in Illinois and the other in Ontario, Canada. The Canadian center rehabilitated only owls. I did take some random courses at University of New Hampshire for a couple of years. I studied biology, zoology, ornithology, and wildlife management.

Q: How did you get your first job as a rehabilitator?

A: I heard about a wildlife center in Massachusetts from a friend of mine. Since I was living in New Hampshire, it was the closest center that actually hired paid staff. I was very persistent with the director, and called once a week asking if there was anything I could do. After about two months, he called to say they had an opening for a weekend clinic person. It was an hour-and-a-half drive through Boston, but I was working with wildlife and getting paid for it, so it was a place to start.

I learned how to handle many different species of mammals and birds here, answered questions over the phone, and dealt with the public, who were bringing animals to the center. It was a lot of work and often exhausting (thank goodness I was only 22 at the time!), but I got a good picture of what wildlife rehabilitation was all about.

Q: How did you get your current job?

A: After a year and a half of driving to Massachusetts to work, I decided to look for something closer to home. I heard about a new center getting started in Cape Neddick, Maine, and thought I would go to see what it was all about. It was a fledgling group being run by a veterinarian and volunteers, so I volunteered some time. I didn't have a lot of experience, but I was able to help some of the people who knew very little about the animals. A year later, I was asked to come on board part time to help organize the animal rehabilitation and answer the phone. I've been there ever since.

Q: *What do you like most about your job?*
A: I would have to say I like the chance to be able to work with the hundreds of different species of birds and animals we see every year. It is not every day someone can be up close to hummingbirds, red-tailed hawks, great blue herons, red squirrels, porcupines, barred owls, and other wildlife. Also, the thrill of releasing a rehabilitated animal back into the wild is by far the most rewarding part of the job.

Q: *What do you like least about it?*
A: Seeing so many animals injured because of humans encroaching on their habitats as well as having to euthanize the animals that cannot be rehabilitated.

Q: *What is a typical workday for you?*
A: In the summer my day starts pretty early. Usually I go in about 7:00 A.M. to start feeding baby birds and clean. Because I have two young children, I go home to get them ready to head off for the day and return to the center around 10:30 A.M. to help clean, medicate, and examine the dozens of animals at the center. The phone is very busy in the summer, so I spend a great deal of time talking with people who have encountered an animal and are looking for advice. There is very little time to even stop and eat lunch during the busy months!

There are days when we have to transport many animals to the veterinarian that need to be examined or put down, and this often takes 2 to 2½ hours including travel time. A good day will end around 4:00 or 4:30 P.M., but there are days I have to go back to the center after picking up my kids to check on animals or to help close up, which happens at about 9:00 P.M. during summer months.

Q: What is the most important aspect to your job?
A: Overseeing the operations of the center, examining animals that have just been admitted to the center, and determining treatment or prognosis.

Q: What advice do you have for those who are considering wildlife rehabilitation as a career?
A: Make sure you are ready to commit most of your time and life to the job. Wildlife rehabilitation is very consuming and it takes a tremendous amount of physical and emotional energy. Learn how to balance work and personal life to avoid getting burned out too fast. Focus on the animals that you have been able to help, not the ones that you cannot, since this is usually out of your control.

ZOOKEEPER

Zoos were once places where people simply went to view exotic animals; today, these institutions are much more than that. They are facilities where endangered species are kept alive and encouraged to reproduce, and where the public is taught the value of wildlife conservation.

The individuals responsible for taking care of the animals that live in zoos are traditionally known as zookeepers. Once a job consisting only of cleaning after and feeding of animals, the job of zookeeper has become much more complex and rewarding.

Zookeepers are still in charge of making sure that animals are well fed and cared for, but their duties also involve educating the public, participating in research, training animals, designing exhibits, and more.

Because the role of zookeeper has broadened from that of simple caretaker to a more complicated position, zoos today are showing a preference for hiring individuals with college degrees. However, prospective zookeepers with extensive experience handling zoo animals along with some formal schooling (but no degree) are still considered.

While large metropolitan zoos are some of the bigger employers of zookeepers, smaller zoos in suburban and rural locations also require the services of animal caretakers.

WHAT ZOOKEEPERS DO

Typical duties of a zookeeper are:

- daily care of animals in a particular part of the zoo if the facility is large, in all areas of the zoo if the facility is small; includes feeding, watering, and cage cleaning of a variety of different species

- observing animals daily for signs of illness or injury

- assisting in building or planning exhibits

- caring for infant mammals that were rejected or removed from the mother

- involvement in educational programs for the public

About the Profession

- The American Association of Zoo Keepers (AAZK) is a professional organization dedicated to the career of zookeeping.
- Nearly 5,000 zookeepers are employed in the United States.
- Many zookeepers belong to a zookeepers' union.
- Obtaining volunteer experience in zoos is one of the best qualifications for the job of professional zookeeper.

WHAT THE JOB IS *REALLY* LIKE

Zookeepers spend most of their time working outdoors in all kinds of weather. Their job entails working evenings, weekends, and holidays, although most put in only about 40 hours a week.

Because a big part of the zookeeper's responsibility is cleaning up after zoo animals, the job can get messy and smelly. Heavy lifting is often required as well. Zoo environments are often noisy, so zoo employees have to contend with this as well.

Zookeepers must often deal with the public, not all of whom are respectful and well behaved around the animals. The animals in the zookeeper's charge are not always well behaved either, and zookeepers are at risk for being bitten, kicked, and scratched. They also have to cope with the realities of death when an animal they have grown attached to has died from illness or old age.

WHY BECOME A ZOOKEEPER?

Although taking care of zoo animals is hard work, the rewards to this job are many:

- knowing you are providing exotic and sometimes endangered animals with good care

- the chance to work closely with exotic animals on a daily basis

- helping animals that are sick or injured

- educating the public on the importance of wildlife conservation

- participating in breeding and conservation programs

TRAITS YOU'LL NEED

- a love of animals and a strong desire to work with them

- a knowledge of animal behavior, husbandry, and wildlife

- good communication skills and willingness to work with the public

- patience with animals that may not always be cooperative

- reliability and dedication to caring for animals

- a desire for continued learning

- good physical health

- a willingness to risk being injured by an animal

TRAINING AND CERTIFICATION

More and more zookeeper positions are requiring four-year college degrees. However, a high school diploma or GED along with extensive volunteer experience with zoo animals and some college or continuing education courses in animal science, animal behavior, zoology, conservation biology, and wildlife management can substitute. Prior experience as a veterinary technician or wildlife rehabilitator can also be helpful in procuring a job in this competitive field.

EARNINGS

The amount of money a zookeeper earns depends on the particular zoo he or she works for and where the facility is located. Larger zoos in urban areas tend to pay more than smaller, local zoos. It's not uncommon for an entry-level zookeeper to start at minimum wage, or range from $25,000 or more a year. Experienced keepers can make $30,000 a year or more.

A FEW KEY POINTS TO REMEMBER

• The first step to most careers with wildlife is volunteer work. Be prepared to spend a year or more as a volunteer in the profession you hope to pursue.

• Although jobs with wildlife involve dealing with animals, interacting with humans is also an important element as well. Make sure you have good people skills as well as skills at handling animals.

• Long hours and low pay are common in careers dealing with wildlife. Be certain you are willing to work for minimal pay before pursuing one of these jobs.

Resources

Resources

PROFESSIONAL AND BUSINESS ORGANIZATIONS

General

Cat Fanciers Association, Inc.
P.O. Box 1005
Manasquan, NJ 08736-0805
(732) 528-9797
www.cfainc.org

Horse Industry Alliance
P.O. Box 56
Bertram, TX 78605
(512) 355-3225
www.horseindustryalliance.com

American Horse Council
1700 K Street, NW
Suite 300
Washington, DC 20006-3805
(202) 296-4031
www.horsecouncil.org

American Professional Pet Distributors, Inc.
(APPDI)
440 Pinburr lane
Stone Mountain, GA 30087
(404) 498-5984

Pet Industry Distributors Association (PIDA)
5024-R Campbell Road
Baltimore, MD 21236
(301) 256-8100
www.pida.org

Professional Association of Pet Industries
4311 Treat Boulevard
Concord, CA 94521
(415) 674-0500

Animal Control Officer

National Animal Control Association
P.O. Box 480851
Kansas City, MO 64148
(913) 768-0607
www.nacanet.org

American Humane Association
63 Inverness Dr. E.
Englewood, CO 80112
(303) 792-9900
www.americanhumane.org

Aquarist

Marine Aquarium Society of North America,
Inc.
c/o David Adkins
15791 Bowfin Blvd.
Brookpark, OH 44142
masna.org

Boarding Kennel Manager

American Boarding Kennels Association
4575 Galley Rd., Suite 400A
Colorado Springs, CO 80915
(719) 591-1113
www.abka.com

American Pet Boarding Association
P.O. Box 931
Wheeling, IL 60090
(312) 634-9447

Dog Trainer

National Association of Dog Obedience
Instructors
PMB # 369
729 Grapevine Hwy, Suite 369
Hurst, TX 76054-2085
www.nadoi.org

The Association of Pet Dog Trainers
66 Morris Ave., Ste. 2A
Springfield, NJ 07081
(800) PET-DOGS
www.apdt.com

Equine Massage Therapist

International Association of Equine Sports
Massage Therapists
P.O. Box 447
Round Hill, VA 20141
www.iaesmt.com

Equissage
P.O. Box 447
Round Hill, VA 20142
(800) 843-0224
www.equissage.com

Farrier

American Farriers Association
4059 Iron Works Pike
Lexington, KY 40511-8434
(859) 233-7411
www.amfarriers.com

Groomer

National Dog Groomers Association
Box 101
Clark, PA 16113
(412) 962-2711
www.nauticom.net/www/ndga
(for a listing of state-licensed grooming
schools, send stamped, self-addressed
envelope)

American Grooming Shop Association
4575 Galley Road, #400A
Colorado Springs, CO 80915
(719) 570-7788

Northwest Professional Groomers Association
10220 29th St. E. #5
Puyallup, WA 98372
(206) 841-2544

Park Ranger

National Park Service Headquarters
Robert Stanton, Director
National Park Service
1849 C Street NW
Washington, DC 20240
(202) 208-6843
www.nps.gov

Pet Sitter

Pet Sitters International
418 East King Street
King, NC 27021-9163
(336) 983-9222
www.petsit.com

National Association of Professional Pet
Sitting
1200 G St. NW, Suite 760
Washington, DC 20005
(202) 393-3317
www.petsitters.org

Pet Sitters Associates, LLC
4014 Boardwalk St.
Eau Claire, WI 54701
(800) 872-2941, access code 25
www.petsitllc.com

International Association of Home Pet Care
Services
38 Sunset Drive
Kensington, CA 94707
(415) 524-0451

Professional Handler

American Kennel Club
5580 Centerview Drive
Raleigh, NC 27606-3390
(919) 233-9767
www.akc.org

Professional Handlers Association
15810 Mt. Everest Lane
Silver Spring, MD 20906
(301) 924-0089

Dog Handlers Guild
413 Dempsey Avenue SW
Buffalo, MN 55313
(612) 682-3366
www.infodog.com/misc/dhg/dhgmain.htm

Riding Instructor

The British Horse Society
Stoneleigh Deer Park
Kenilworth
Warwickshire. CV8 2XZ
Tel. 08701 202 244
www.bhs.org.uk
e-mail: A.Bingle@bhs.org.uk

American Association for Horsemanship Safety,
Inc.
Golondrina Stables
P.O. Drawer 39
Fentress, TX 78622
(512) 488-2220
www.law.utexas.edu/dawson

United States Dressage Federation
P.O. Box 6669
Lincoln, NE 68506-0669
(402) 434-8550
www.usdf.org

American Riding Instructors Association
28801 Trenton Court
Bonita Springs, FL 34134
(941) 948-3232
www.win.net/aria

United States Pony Clubs, Inc.
4071 Iron Works Pike
Lexington, KY 40511-8462
(606) 254-PONY
ponyclub.org

American Riding Instructor Certification
Program
P.O. Box 282
Alton Bay, NH 03810-0282
(603) 875-4000

North American Riding for the Handicapped
P.O. Box 33150
Denver, CO 80233
(800) 369-RIDE
www.narha.org

Certified Horsemanship Association
5318 Old Bullard
Tyler, TX 70503
(800) 399-0138
www.cha-ahse.org

TTEAM Training International
P.O. Box 3793
Santa Fe, NM 87501-0793
(505) 455-2945
tteam-ttouch.com

Shelter Worker

The Humane Society of the United States
2100 L St. NW.
Washington, DC 20037-1598
www.hsus.org

Veterinary Technician/Assistant

American Veterinary Medical Association
930 N. Meacham Road
Schaumburg, IL 60196
(800) 248-2862
www.avma.org
(info on veterinary technician certification)

North American Veterinary Technicians
Association
P.O. Box 224
Battle Ground, IN 47920
(317) 742-2216
www.avma.org/navta

American Association for Laboratory Animal
Science
9190 Crestwyn Hills Drive
Memphis, TN 38125
www.aalas.org

Wildlife Rehabilitator

National Wildlife Rehabilitators Association
14 North 7 Avenue
St. Cloud, MN 56303
(320) 259-4086
www.nwrawildlife.org

International Wildlife Rehabilitation Council
4437 Central Place, Suite B-4
Suisun City, CA 94585
(707) 864-1761
www.iwrc-online.org

Wrangler

Dude Ranchers' Association
P.O. Box F-471
LaPorte, CO 80535
(970) 223-8440
www.duderanch.org

Zookeeper

Association of Zoo and Aquarium Docents
Sue Kiebler, Columbus Zoological Gardens
P.O. Box 400
Powell, OH 43065-0400
(614) 645-3400
www.azadocents.org

American Association of Zoo Keepers
3601 S.W. 29th St., Suite 133
Topeka, KS 66614
aazk.ind.net

American Zoo and Aquarium Association
8403 Colesville Rd., Suite 710
Silver Spring, MD 20910-3314
(301) 562-0777
www.aza.org

ANIMAL MAGAZINES

Dog Publications

AKC Gazette
American Kennel Club
51 Madison Avenue
New York, NY 10010

Dog Fancy
Fancy Publications
P.O. Box 6050
Mission Viejo, CA 92690

Dog World
P.O. Box 6500
Chicago, IL 60680

Dogs in Canada
Canadian Kennel Club
89 Skyway Ave., Suite 200
Etobicoke, Ontario M9Q 6R4
Canada

Dogs U.S.A.
Fancy Publications
P.O. Box 6050
Mission Viejo, CA 92690

Dogs in Canada Annual
Canadian Kennel Club
89 Skyway Ave., Suite 200
Etobicoke, Ontario M9Q 6R4
Canada

Groom & Board
H.H. Backer Associates Inc.
200 S. Michigan Ave., Suite 840
Chicago, IL 60604
(312) 663-4040

Horse Publications

Horse Illustrated
P.O. Box 6050
Mission Viejo, CA 92690
(949) 855-8822
www.animalnetwork.com/horses

Equus
656 Quince Orchard Rd., Suite 600
Gaithersburg, MD 20878
(301) 977-3900

Horses U.S.A.
P.O. Box 6050
Mission Viejo, CA 92690
(949) 855-8822

Horse and Rider
1597 Cole Boulevard, Suite 350
Golden, CO 80401
(800) 829-3340

Practical Horseman
6405 Flank Drive
Harrisburg, PA 17112
(800) 829-3340

Cat Publications

Cat Fancy
Fancy Publications
P.O. Box 6050
Mission Viejo, CA 92690
(949) 855-8822

Cats U.S.A.
Fancy Publications
P.O. Box 6050
Mission Viejo, CA 92690
(949) 855-8822

Cats Magazine
260 Madison Avenue, 8th Floor
New York, NY 10016
(917) 256-2305

Wildlife Publications

Wildlife Rehabilitation Today
Coconut Creek Publishing Company
2201 NW 40th Terrace
Coconut Creek, FL 33066-2032
(954) 977-5058

Aquarium Maintenance Business Guide
AquaServe Aquarium Publications
1210 Colonial Hills Dr.
Mobile, AL 36695
ContactUs@aquaserve.com

Index